THE SOUL OF A TEAM

THE
SOUL
OF A
TEAM

**A MODERN-DAY FABLE
FOR WINNING TEAMWORK**

TONY DUNGY
WITH NATHAN WHITAKER

*The nonfiction imprint of
Tyndale House Publishers, Inc.*

Library of Congress Cataloging-in-Publication Data
Names: Dungy, Tony, author.
Title: The soul of a team : a modern-day fable for winning teamwork / Tony Dungy with Nathan Whitaker.
Description: Carol Stream, Illinois : Tyndale House Publishers, Inc., 2018. | Includes bibliographical references.
Identifiers: LCCN 2018036561 | ISBN 9781496413765 (hc)
Subjects: LCSH: Teams in the workplace. | Leadership.
Classification: LCC HD66 .D86 2018 | DDC 658.4/022—dc23 LC record available at https://lccn.loc.gov/2018036561

Printed in the United States of America

24   23   22   21   20   19   18
7   6   5   4   3   2   1

CONTENTS

Author's Note

I HAVE BEEN WORKING in or around the National Football League for more than forty years—first as a player for the Pittsburgh Steelers and San Francisco 49ers, then as a coach for the Pittsburgh Steelers, Kansas City Chiefs, Minnesota Vikings, Tampa Bay Buccaneers, and Indianapolis Colts, and now as a broadcast analyst for NBC. In that time, I have seen some pretty crazy stuff: tantrums, arrests, locker room fights, leaks to reporters about personnel issues, you name it. I've also seen a lot of great things: selfless acts of courage and compassion, moments of kindness and humility, and people living with faith and integrity and making a genuine difference in the world.

Though some individuals behave horribly and others live honorably, they all have something in common: They affect the people around them. The same is true of us. Our actions and attitudes really do impact those we live and work with. No wonder the number one topic I'm asked to speak about is teamwork.

I've spent decades considering what it takes for a team to rise to the top. I've learned that talent alone isn't enough; some teams that appear most promising on paper end up fizzling. Through experience—both successes and failures—I have learned what generally separates high-achieving teams from those that fail to produce.

After I was invited to write a book on this topic, one of the first decisions I needed to make was how to best present this information to you. Given that I've spent two-thirds of my life on or around football teams, I decided the most natural approach would be to unpack these principles through a story set in the environment I'm most familiar with. In addition, I hope reading about teamwork in this context will be interesting and fun for you. And while the context may be set in professional football, these principles apply to *all* teams, whether within a family unit, a company or church, or a high school drama club.

All characters and events associated with the Orlando Vipers, the fictitious expansion team around which the story centers, are imaginary. To help explain principles, I sometimes draw upon actual people and incidents I have observed—both on my own teams and others'—over the past four decades.

Tony Dungy

PART I

The Problem

THE CALL

ON A PICTURE-PERFECT FEBRUARY DAY IN TAMPA, I was out in the yard hitting grounders and pop flies to my son Justin. I had just gotten back from the Super Bowl in Miami, where Chicago, in an ending for the ages, had beaten Baltimore on a game-ending pick-six.

"Stay in front of it, Justin," I called out as he raced forward to stop a hard grounder. "Try not to play it off to the side if you can help it."

Upon running it down, he snatched the ball up in his glove, stood, and hurled it back. As the ball smacked into my bare palm, I could literally feel his frustration. "Hey, easy there," I said. "Remember, I'm not wearing a glove."

"Sorry," he mumbled, turning away.

I took a second to shake off the sting. Poor kid. A natural lefty, he had wanted to play first base, but after seeing his speed, the coach decided to put him in center field. To Justin's credit, he was giving it his all and doing very well. Practically every game, he saved a couple of runs by chasing a ball down or making a great catch.

But Justin didn't see it that way. In fact, on our drive home from practice just a few days before, he had slumped down in the backseat and told me he hated his coach.

"Why?" I asked. "Your coach is a great guy."

"Because," he grumbled, "he won't let me play first base. I hate the outfield."

On the one hand, I got it. Pretty much every Little League kid wants to play in the infield or pitch. I know I did when I was his age. Still, I wanted to hear his reasoning.

"Why do you want to play first base?"

"Because that's where all the action is," he said matter-of-factly. "In center field, I only get like two balls a game, tops. If I was playing first base, I'd get fifteen or twenty."

"You know why the coach has you out there, don't you?" I asked.

"Yeah . . . he hates me," he shot back.

"He doesn't hate you, Justin," I said, catching his eye in the rearview mirror. "Yes, 90 percent of the balls are hit in the infield, but if someone does hit one into the outfield, your team's going to give up a lot of runs if it's not caught. You're the fastest one on that team. You can cover a lot of ground out there—maybe more than anyone else. That's why he's got you in center. You're playing a very important position. He put you there because it's what's best for the team."

I could almost see the gears spinning in his ten-year-old mind as he turned his attention to the scenery whizzing by. *He'll get it—eventually*, I consoled myself.

But two days later, back in our yard, he was still upset.

"Okay, Justin," I said, tossing the ball a little higher. "Let's see some of that speed!" The bat sent the ball up into the air about fifteen yards to Justin's left. Without hesitating, he took off like a shot, reached across his body, and made a spectacular backhand grab.

"See? That's what I'm talking about!"

"Tony!" my wife, Lauren, called from the patio. "Terry Hodges is on the phone."

"Back in a minute, buddy," I said to Justin. Even though he was a good thirty feet away, I could see him roll his eyes. He knew by now that whenever a friend from the NFL called, it was rarely just a minute.

•　　•　　•　　•　　•

I hadn't spoken with Terry in weeks—not since his Orlando Vipers had missed the playoffs with a loss to Dallas in the final game of the regular season.

"I'll take it in my study," I said to Lauren as I passed her in the kitchen.

She smiled, winked at me, and nodded her head toward Justin in the backyard. "How's he doing today?"

"He's still a little upset, but he'll come around."

Lauren sighed. "I hope so."

"Hey, Terry," I said after picking up the phone in my office. "It's good to hear from you. How's everything in Orlando?"

"Hi, Tony. About as can be expected, I guess." He sounded tired, defeated. But then so did the other team presidents, except for one, now that the season was over and they hadn't won the Super Bowl.

"I have to tell you, Terry . . . I really thought you guys were going to make it into the playoffs this year." And I meant that. After Terry had left his position as a federal judge to take over the reins of the Vipers, I could sense they were on the cusp of something great. But like a lot of teams, too many mistakes, injuries, bad luck, and bad plays eventually caught up with them.

"Yeah, so did I," he said, sighing. "That's what I wanted to talk to you about."

"Sure," I said, settling in at my desk. "What's up?"

Terry paused for a second, then spoke, his words uncharacteristically tumbling over themselves. "I don't know what to do here, Tony. We just can't seem to turn the corner. I've been here three seasons now, and we've gone 8–8, 7–9, and now 8–8 again. The owner's frustrated, the coaches are frustrated, the players are frustrated, the fans are frustrated . . ."

"And *you're* frustrated," I said, finishing the sentence for him.

"Yes," he replied, the tone of defeat clear in his voice.

Football. It's all fun and games when you're winning, I mused, leaning back in my chair. *But when you're not . . .*

Terry was just getting started. "Frankly, Tony, I've about given up on this group. In fact, I'm thinking about just blowing the whole thing up, firing everyone, and starting over from scratch."

Now *that* caught my attention. I'd known Terry for almost ten years, and he'd always been a very measured, deliberate, and thoughtful guy—definitely not the type to go off half-cocked and start firing people on a dime.

I sat back up. "Seriously? You'd fire Gym? And Joe? That's a little rash, isn't it? Gym McKenzie is a fantastic person, Terry. And from what I can tell, an excellent general manager. He's put together very talented teams, both for you in Orlando and in Detroit a few years ago.

"As for Joe Webster," I continued, "I've only spent a little time with him since he became head coach, but he seems like a solid person. It's only been a couple of seasons, Terry. You've got to give the guy a chance."

"I hear you, Tony," Terry replied, "but something's got to give. The team's going nowhere. We've spent a ton on players and brought in the best coaching staff we could find, but it doesn't feel like we're making any progress. We should be so much better than we are.

"The really aggravating thing," he said, "is that we beat three of the teams that made it to the playoffs this year by ten points or more, including New England—on the road! We were even the last team to beat Chicago before they went on their Super Bowl run."

"Yeah, that was a great game . . ." I was about to continue when Terry cut me off.

"But then we turned right around and lost back-to-back games to teams scraping the bottoms of their divisions. We've got some of the best talent in this league, and yet we can't seem to maintain any sense of consistency."

I tried to defuse the situation a little. "Listen, Terry. Firing everyone is rarely the right move. Bear in mind that as bad as things seem, there are easily ten or twelve other teams that would love to have your problems. I think you're really close."

"I know," Terry conceded. "But even with a top-five offense and a top-twenty defense, we're still trapped in the middle. Fifteenth—in a league where only the top twelve make the playoffs."

I had to admit he was making some excellent points. The Vipers had a lot of talented players and, from what I could tell, a top-notch coaching staff. And sure, sometimes challenging times call for drastic measures. But the concept of mass firings has never sat well with me. For one thing, you run the risk of losing some good people along with the bad. It also creates an environment of fear and mistrust among those left behind, which is rarely productive. More important, though, firing people in an organization affects not only *them* but their families as well. It's just not the kind of decision good leaders take lightly—or make in haste out of desperation.

"Listen, Terry, before you fire anyone . . ."

"That's why I'm calling, Tony," he interrupted. "I don't *want* to fire anyone. At least not unless I absolutely have to. In fact," he paused for a second, "I'm thinking of *hiring* someone."

"Who?" I asked.

"You."

I tried—and failed—to stifle a laugh. "Terry, I'm officially retired. You know that. My coaching days are over. Besides, Lauren would have my head if—"

"No, no, no. I'm not talking about coaching, Tony. I'm talking about consulting. Just come out to the facility a couple of days a week. You are only about an hour away, so whatever your schedule allows. Sit in on team meetings, staff meetings, practices. I'll even clear out an office for you so players, coaches, and other staff can drop in and chat with you."

"About what?" I asked.

"Whatever they'd like," he said. "Look, Tony, I need to get a fresh perspective on this. Maybe you can tell us what's wrong. Do I need to fire someone? Everyone? Is the problem the players, the coaching staff, or both? Or maybe we have all the right pieces and they're just not fitting together. I really could use a fresh set of eyes here. What do you say?"

"I don't know. It's tough to get involved as an outsider and not make a mess of things," I cautioned.

"Things are already a mess," Terry said. "That's why I'm calling. I don't expect you to have all the answers, but you *have* been around this league for a long time, and you've worked with some of the best in the business. If anyone can tell me what we're doing wrong and help steer us in the right direction, it's you."

"Wait a minute, Terry," I interrupted him. "Don't give me too much credit. Anything I've done right over the course of my career is just a reflection of things I've learned from people like Chuck Noll, Denny Green, and Bill Walsh. Those guys had a *huge* influence on me."

"I know, Tony. There's no question you've learned from the best. And our guys could really benefit from that. What good is all your knowledge if you don't pass it on?"

Now he had me. I owed practically everything I'd accomplished to those guys, as well as to others who had mentored me. It did seem like a shame not to pass it on.

As I leaned back in my chair, I caught a glimpse of Justin out in the yard tossing the ball to himself. A smile crept across my face. Even the advice I'd given him the other day in the car was inspired by what Coach Noll had told me when I first joined the Steelers: "Every job on this team is important!"

"Well?" Terry nudged. "What do you say, Tony?"

I had to admit, the idea was intriguing. *It would only be a few hours a week,* I reasoned. I glanced over at a framed picture of me and Denny Green after a Colts-Cardinals game. *He's right,* I thought. *Some advice is just too good to keep to yourself.*

"Well, Lauren and I will have to discuss it first, but if she's on board . . . frankly, Terry, I would love to help."

• • • • •

As expected, getting Lauren to agree to the idea wasn't easy. She had been a coach's wife long enough to know that a couple of hours a week could quickly turn into a couple of hours a day, possibly more. Terry even came out to the house to promise her in person that my involvement with the team would be temporary and mostly confined to the off-season. In other words, he wasn't asking me to take on a full-time job—just spend a couple of days at the stadium here and there to observe, listen, and offer some advice.

"Then why does he need an office?" she asked.

"Simply for privacy," Terry assured her. "I want our players and coaches to feel as though they can confide in Tony—speak freely with him about their concerns—and that's hard to do in a crowded locker room or hallway.

"Trust me," he continued, "I know how important family time is to the two of you, and I have no intention of disrupting that. And I wouldn't even be asking if I hadn't already exhausted every other viable option."

Lauren remained unpersuaded. Terry glanced at me in desperation, but I just smiled. Then Terry turned back to her and threw a final Hail Mary.

"Tell you what. What if we all agree that the minute this position becomes an inconvenience for you, Tony, or the kids, we call it a day?"

Lauren looked over at me. I raised my eyebrows and smiled. She knew how much I liked and admired Terry—we both did. She also knew how much it would mean to me to be able to help a friend in need.

The corners of her mouth turned up slightly, and then she looked back at Terry.

"Okay," she managed, exhaling deeply. "We'll *try* it."

Welcome to the Viper Pit

After dropping the kids off at school the following Monday, I drove up to Orlando to meet with Terry, Gym McKenzie, Joe Webster, and the Vipers' owner, Owen Joyce. At Terry's request, I met him at one of the stadium's side doors.

"Hey, Tony, welcome to Serpent World's Viper Pit Stadium," Terry said.

"I haven't been to this stadium in a long time," I said. "A few college games are still played here every year, right?"

"Yep," Terry said. "And concerts, an occasional soccer game, and even an annual rodeo. Technically the city owns the stadium. We're just tenants.

"I hope you don't mind skipping the main entrance," he apologized as he ushered me inside. "After Harding's column ran yesterday, I don't want to give the rumor mill any unnecessary fodder."

"I understand completely," I assured him. I had seen the column myself. It was hard to miss—front and center on page 1 of the *Orlando Press* sports section. The well-known columnist had penned a scathing piece calling for Joe Webster's immediate firing. A new head coach, he argued, was critical to getting the Vipers over the hump and fans back in the seats.

Having been on the chopping block myself once, I couldn't help but feel for Joe. *Why does everyone always assume it's the coach's fault?* I wondered.

I followed Terry down a hallway lined with photos of memorable moments from the team's inaugural season, most of them featuring the star wide receiver, Wickie Ariet. The white walls stood in stark contrast to the jet-black carpeting with thin lime-green stripes and gold diamonds. *Now that had to have been custom-made,* I thought. *I can't imagine anyone having* this *design in stock.*

"Snakeskin," Terry explained, catching my eye. "Get it?"

"Got it," I chuckled.

"So where would you like to start?" he asked.

"Owen, if he's available," I responded.

"Straight to the top, huh?" Terry said, smiling as he held his ID badge up to the electronic pad next to the door. The lock snapped open.

"He's the vision caster," I said. Terry looked at me as though he had something to say, but he just kept walking instead. I thought about asking him if there was anything he wanted to tell me but then decided against it. Whatever I needed to know about the man at the top, I'd find out soon enough.

• • • • •

Two short hallways and an elevator ride later, we found ourselves outside the office of Owen Joyce, owner of the Orlando Vipers.

When the heavy double wooden doors swung open, we were greeted by an impeccably dressed man in his midsixties with a broad face and graying hair. He had the large-but-soft torso of a man who had retained muscle after years of physical exercise yet gained a layer of heft from too many business dinners.

"Coach Dungy, so nice to finally meet you!" he boomed, giving my hand a vigorous shake.

"It's nice to meet you, too, Mr. Joyce," I returned. "But please call me Tony."

"Only if you call me Owen," he replied, letting go of my hand. "Terry, will you be joining us?"

"Actually, I have a few things I need to take care of," Terry said, checking his watch. "Besides, I'm sure you two have a lot to talk about. Tony, I'll see you later, okay?"

"Sounds good, Terry." I managed to add a quick "Thanks" before the doors swung shut.

"Make yourself at home, Tony," Owen offered, welcoming me in.

"Thank you," I said. Owen's office was bright and spacious, with an entire wall of floor-to-ceiling windows that provided an unobstructed view of the playing field below. Opposite the windows sat a massive mahogany desk with two large, overstuffed leather chairs facing it. The wall behind the desk showcased photos of Owen posing next to an assortment of celebrities and politicians—including the last three presidents—as well as plaques denoting various honors and awards and framed covers of *Forbes*, *Fortune 500*, and *Money* magazines featuring stories about Owen. Beside the desk stood an empty, six-foot-tall mahogany trophy case that had a single light radiating from the top onto a glass shelf about a third of the way down. I must have stared at it longer than I thought because before I knew it, Owen was standing next to me, his right hand on my shoulder.

"I had this built special," he said, "for my first Lombardi."

"It's a beautiful case," I said.

"Beautiful . . . but empty," he countered, walking toward his desk. "That's why you're here." As he sat down, he gestured to one of the oversized leather chairs.

"Well . . . ," I started, sinking so deeply into the chair that I wasn't sure I could get up without help, "I can't make any promises. I'm just here to get a sense of your organization—see what's working, what's not—and hopefully provide some helpful advice."

"Listen," Owen said, leaning forward. "I'm all for whatever will win games and make money. I'm serious. I'll try anything—firings, restructurings, trades, forced retirements—whatever it takes. I've sunk a lot of money into this organization over the past three years, and it's time I started seeing results. You're not looking at a man who's accustomed to losing." I was beginning to get a sense of why Terry had contemplated firing his entire coaching staff. Clearly he was getting a lot of pressure from the top to produce results—immediately.

"I understand that," I said, keeping my voice soothing. "And I'll tell you the same thing I told Terry. You've got a lot of good people in this organization, Owen, and a lot of talented players. This team's only been together for a couple of seasons. Sometimes it takes time for everyone to gel."

"Time, Tony," Owen said, steepling his fingers, "is a luxury we don't have. We're only three years in, and our attendance is already starting to drop off. If things keep going the way they're going, the league's going to start blacking out our home games. That means no ad revenue," he said, pushing his chair back and rising to his full six-and-a-half-foot frame. "I need to turn things around now!"

Once again I found myself trying to talk a panicky executive off the ledge. "Okay, slow down," I said. He was becoming excitable, but for the life of me, I could *not* get out of that chair. I waited, and after a moment, he sat back down. "I get it. At the end of the day, football is a business. And just like any other corporation, you've got to keep your consumer base happy, or you go under. And sure, *part* of the way you do that is by putting a good product on the field—"

"*Part* of it?" he interrupted.

"Yes." I paused for a second and continued. "Let me ask you this. What is the mission for this team? In other words, what do you want to accomplish?"

"To win the Super Bowl," he shot back in a tone that implied I was a lunatic for even asking.

"That's it?" I asked.

"Of course that's it," he snapped. "What else is there?"

"You finished 8–8 this season," I said. "What if you were to make the playoffs next year? Would you consider that a success?"

He stared at me incredulously. "Just the playoffs?"

"Just the playoffs," I confirmed.

"What's the point of making it to the playoffs if you don't get to the big game?"

I could tell he was starting to get irritated.

"Okay," I conceded. "Let's say you make it to the big game— and you lose."

He leaned back in his chair, tilted his head to the right, and stared at me. "What are you getting at, Tony?"

"What I'm getting at is this. Getting to the Super Bowl—"

"*Winning* the Super Bowl," he interrupted.

"*Winning* the Super Bowl," I corrected, "is a great goal. But if that's the *only* goal you have for this organization, you're setting your team up for failure."

"Are you saying we can't win?" he challenged.

"No, I'm not saying that at all. All I'm saying is that there are more than thirty teams in this league, and if the only way you measure success is by winning the Super Bowl, then all but one of those teams—many of which will have experienced tremendous improvement over the course of the season and achieved things they've never done before—would be failures by your measure. That's not good for morale—in *any* industry."

"Neither is losing," he shot back.

"This is true," I agreed. "But there are ways for organizations to define success other than a Super Bowl win."

I started to sense that I was losing him, so I decided to shift gears.

"Let me ask you another question. Where do you see this team in three years?"

"Honestly?" he asked.

"Honestly."

A subtle smile crept across his face. "Oakland."

Whoa. I didn't see that *coming.*

"Really? Why do you say that?" I asked.

Owen stood and walked over to the glass wall overlooking the stadium. "Look at this place, Tony," he said, gesturing down at the stands. "This stadium is old and outdated, and we've got one of the lowest seating capacities in the league."

I couldn't argue with him there. It *was* one of the oldest stadiums in the league. I'd also heard from friends that the fan experience at Vipers games left a lot to be desired.

"I agree—a nicer stadium would be great. But why not build something here? Why take the team someplace else?"

He shrugged. "Like I said, attendance is already down. There's no way the city is going to foot the bill for a new state-of-the-art stadium—especially when we can't even make it into the wild card mix."

"So you'd just up and move the team to Oakland?" I asked.

"Why not? You said it yourself. We've only been here a few years. The Vipers don't have any more attachment to this city than they have to us."

If it weren't physically impossible, I was almost sure I sank even deeper into my chair.

"What about your coaching staff, the players, and all the other people you've got working here?" I asked. "What about the fans?"

"Look," he said, "don't get me wrong. I love Orlando. I was born here, raised here. I've raised my own kids here. This is a great city. That's why I started this team in the first place. But something's not working, Tony. I don't know what it is, but something's missing. If you can help us turn this ship around and we can start winning some games . . . great. That'll bring the fans back around, and *maybe* we'll have a shot at a new stadium."

I sensed there was a *but* coming.

"But," he continued, "if we can't fix this thing and fast—"

"California, here we come," I finished.

Owen smiled, snapped his fingers, and pointed at me. "Now you're getting it."

Yeah. I got it all right.

• • • • •

"So how'd it go?" Terry asked, his eyes hopeful.

I chose my words carefully. "It was . . . informative."

He shot me a knowing smile and dropped his pen onto the mass of papers he'd been studying. "I figured it would be."

I couldn't help but notice how much smaller, darker, and less opulent Terry's office was than Owen's. It reminded me a little of my first office with the Steelers. Of course, I was only an assistant coach helping out with defensive backs. Terry was the president of an NFL team.

"Well," he said, rising from his chair, "I hate to see you jump from the frying pan into the fire, but I believe Joe Webster is waiting for you down the hall." Gesturing toward the door, he asked, "Shall we?"

"Can't wait," I laughed.

At the end of the hall stood a pair of large wooden doors with a giant snake's head carved across them, its fangs protruding to the left. "That's a little ominous," I joked.

Terry winked at me. "Wait till you meet Joe."

"Should I be worried?" I asked.

"No. But *he* might be," he said as we passed the huge doors leading to the team locker room. "He's been under some pretty heavy scrutiny from the media ever since the Dallas loss. Then Harding's column hit."

"And now *I* show up," I added.

"Exactly. Remember what happened in Washington a few years back?"

I did. I had just retired from the Colts and was working with NBC when the whole thing unfolded. It was a strange situation. The owner had brought in a retired coach and consultant in the middle of the season to help with the offense—a move that was not at all appreciated by the head coach, who had been calling the offensive plays all year. The structure was untenable from the start. Sure enough, the offense completely collapsed, the defense followed suit, and the owner ended up firing the entire coaching staff at the end of the season.

I just shook my head. "Yeah . . . that was a real mess."

"Listen, Joe's a great guy," Terry assured me as we approached Joe's door. "Just don't be surprised if he's not very receptive."

I nodded my head in agreement. "Got it. I wouldn't be, either, if I were in his situation."

As usual, Terry was right. The tension was palpable from the moment we walked into the room. Joe didn't even stand up to greet us but sat hunched behind his desk like a clenched fist, merely looking up and nodding at us. I broke the ice.

"Hey, Joe. It's nice to see you again." I smiled and reached across his cluttered desk with my hand outstretched. After a moment, his hand shook mine.

"Tony," came his one-word greeting.

Following a second or two of awkward silence, Terry broke in. "Well . . . I'm sure you two have a lot of catching up to do." Then he turned to me. "Tony, I'm going to see what I can do about setting up your office somewhere."

"Sounds good, Terry. Thanks," I said, half wishing he'd stay.

After the door closed, I turned my attention to Joe, who was now leaning back in his chair, arms crossed. Terry's comment about getting me an office seemed to have amplified the tension. There was no question about it: This guy was positive I was here to take his job—or at the very least, recommend a replacement.

This could get rough.

Right behind him on the wall were two pictures—one of Joe with Bill Walsh and one with Don Shula. Even though the pictures had to be well over a decade old, Joe's appearance hadn't changed much. The only differences were that now his sandy hair was flecked with gray and his short-sleeved, collared shirt bore the Vipers logo.

"A couple of pretty good Hall of Famers there," I said, nodding at the photos.

He glanced back over his shoulder at the pictures and grunted in agreement. "I was so young and naive back then," he added. "I actually thought I'd be joining them in the Hall myself someday."

"You never know—" I said, taking a seat.

Before I could finish, Joe interjected. "I doubt it. Especially once you've replaced me."

So much for small talk.

"Look, you're a good coach, Joe. You've proven that over

the years. And you've done a lot of really good things here in Orlando." I was completely honest in my assessment. This was Joe's second head coaching stint in the NFL, and before that he'd been an assistant coach for years, both at the college level and in the NFL. He'd coached under some of the best in the business, and the Paul Brown approach to detail and discipline was clear in his teams. He definitely knew his football.

"Listen, Tony," he started, "I know you're here to tell Terry what to do. This isn't my first time around the block. But I'm telling you—" he stood, rested his palms on the edge of his desk, and leaned in—"this is a playoff team next year. The pieces are all in place. We had some tough breaks, some lousy calls, and a few unfortunate injuries this year. We just need to maintain the status quo and catch a couple of breaks, and we'll be right there in the mix."

His statement held some truth. The Vipers had lost two of their best defensive linemen to knee injuries early in the season, their Pro Bowl center had fractured his wrist in the opening drive of the Thanksgiving Day game, and their quarterback had spent the first two weeks of December in concussion protocol.

Of course, in that sense, the Vipers were no different from any other team in the league. No one heads into December with everyone healthy. The difference between playoff-caliber teams and everyone else is the ability to stay the course regardless of the "uncontrollables." Bad breaks—in *any* organization—are inevitable. Bad planning and lack of preparation, however . . .

The cold, hard fact was that three seasons into his tenure as head coach, Joe's record was a lackluster 23–25. Not awful, but certainly not great—and certainly not owed entirely to bad luck.

"I think there are some solid pieces in place, to be sure," I cautiously agreed. "But—"

"But nothing," he said, cutting me off. "I'm not interviewing for my job here, Tony. Either I'm good enough to coach this team or I'm not."

This was going south fast.

"Look, I can't stop guys from getting hurt," he went on, his voice rising almost to a shout. "And I can't control bad calls on the field. I've been in this league a long time, Tony. I can coach. But if you disagree, then go ahead—talk to Terry. Send me on my way, and I'll go hang out at Cocoa Beach for the last two years of my contract." And with that, he sat back down in his chair.

I needed to bring the intensity down a few notches.

"Joe," I said as calmly as possible, "I know you can coach. And just so you know, the whole reason Terry brought me in was because he *doesn't* want to fire anyone. You're right; you can't control everything. Nobody can. Maintaining consistency in the face of adversity is always a challenge. And *succeeding* in the face of adversity . . . well, that's a whole other ball game. And it takes a lot more than raw talent and luck."

That struck a nerve. With his background and the coaches he'd worked for, Joe knew all of this, but it was good for him to hear it from me. Joe took a deep breath, but before he could speak, I pushed forward.

"Listen, Joe. I'm not here to take anyone's job. I'm just trying to help Terry figure out why this team is struggling to break through."

My words changed the calculus for him, but not his stress level. His arms were still folded, his eyes meeting mine. After what seemed an eternity, Joe finally broke the silence.

"Well, when you figure it out, let me know—preferably before another media outlet calls for my head on a platter."

Well . . . I leaned back in my chair. *No pressure there.*

Room for
Improvement

The meeting with Joe left me in need of a little fresh air, so I made my way out onto the field to clear my head and give Lauren a quick call.

"Hey, babe," she said. "How's it going so far?"

After two somewhat explosive meetings, it was nice to hear a calm, comforting voice.

"Well, it's been . . . interesting," I hedged.

"Uh-oh. I don't like the sound of that." I could hear a couple of the kids playing in the background.

"It'll be fine," I assured her. "Is that Justin I hear?"

"Yep. He talked Jason into hitting him some flies."

"Oh, man," I said, trying to imagine our seven-year-old wrangling a bat almost as big as he was. "How's *that* going?"

"It's been . . . interesting," she said as she tried and failed to stifle a laugh. "I tried convincing Justin to move a little closer so Jason wouldn't have to hit so far," she said.

"No dice, though?" I asked, already knowing the answer.

"Nope."

"Well . . . grounders make it into the outfield too."

"Not Jason's," she said. I laughed.

The sound of a door slamming shut behind me caught my attention. When I turned around, I saw Gym McKenzie, the general manager, waving a greeting as he walked toward me. "Listen, Lauren, I've got to run. Tell Justin I'll work with him some more when I get home tonight, okay?" I ended the call just as Gym approached. He looked great—slim, tan, and with a much fuller head of hair than I had at his age.

"Hey, Tony!" he said with a smile. Nodding toward my phone, he added, "I hope I didn't interrupt anything."

"Not at all," I assured him. "I was just checking in with Lauren."

"How *is* Lauren?"

"Good." We had known Gym and his wife, Ellen, for years, though it had been ages since we'd all gotten together.

"And the kids?" he asked.

"They're doing great. Thanks for asking."

"How many now . . . eight? Nine?"

"Ten." I had to admit, sometimes the size of our family took even me by surprise.

"Ten?" he repeated, shaking his head. "Wow. One more and you'd be able to field your own offense!"

"Defense," I noted. "I think we'd field a defense." He laughed. "Actually, that number has held constant for a few years now," I said. "Who knows? Lauren and I may finally be done adopting."

"Well, I can certainly see why Terry brought you in," he remarked. "Anyone who can manage that many kids has to know *something* about running a team."

"It's not all that different," I confessed. "There are a lot of moving pieces, a lot of big personalities, someone's almost always upset about something, and you can go from calm to crisis at the drop of a hat. Fortunately, Lauren and I complement each other really well. She's got her areas of strength and expertise, and I've got mine. But let me tell you, if we aren't always on the same page, delivering the same messages—consistently—across the board . . ."

"Disaster," Gym finished.

"You got it."

"Speaking of disasters, I couldn't help but overhear your conversation with Joe Webster a few minutes ago. Thin walls," he said with a shrug. "Old building."

I still felt bad about how that meeting went. "Yeah. Well, I can certainly understand how he feels. Believe me, I've been in his shoes before, and it's not fun."

"Joe can be a tough nut to crack," he assured me. "He's a good guy, but, well . . . you know how sensitive coaches are." He winked at me. "Present company excepted, of course."

"Of course," I laughed.

"Come on," he said, leading me back toward the building. "Terry mentioned he had to smuggle you in through the side door this morning. I thought you might like the nickel tour."

We passed through the large double doors with the snake's head and walked into the team locker room. Featuring the same black carpet as the hallway, with a giant ten-foot fluorescent-green viper head in the center, it was one of the smallest locker rooms I'd seen. The black carpet, low ceiling, and deep mahogany lockers certainly didn't help it seem any larger.

"It's not quite as spacious as we'd like," Gym said apologetically.

I did a quick count on the lockers. "How many lockers are there in here?"

"Fifty. We were short three, so we keep the specialists in here," he said, leading me over to a small equipment room adjacent to the primary changing area.

"Kicker, punter, and long snapper," he added, pointing to each of the three lockers lining the far wall.

Wow, I thought. *That's pretty rough. Those guys usually already feel like the redheaded stepkids as it is.*

"What about the practice squad?"

Gym nodded to the left. "They're down the hall in the visitors locker room. The ten of them have to clear out their stuff every time we have a home game. We did the best we could, but this stadium simply wasn't built with the daily needs of a modern NFL team in mind."

"That's for sure," I agreed. "If it helps, I've seen worse."

Gym stared at me in disbelief.

"Believe it or not," I said, "our weight room at the old Buccaneers facility was actually outside, under a big vinyl tarp. On rainy days, you could feel the mist blowing in." We both laughed.

"Still," I continued, "it's got to be tough to feel like you're part of the team when you're tucked away in another room or down the hall."

"Agreed," Gym replied, nodding as we started to head back toward the locker room entrance. "But for now, it's all we've got. Frankly, the offices aren't much better. Owen's got a pretty sweet setup, but to be honest, the rest of us are pretty cramped."

"Yeah, I noticed that."

Just as Gym reached the door, it flew open and nearly knocked him over. Wickie Ariet, the star receiver, burst into the room.

"Can you believe this?" he shouted, holding his phone up in front of a still-stunned Gym.

"Wickie," Gym said in the tone of a father correcting his teenage son in public, "I don't believe you've met Coach Dungy."

"Coach." Wickie nodded toward me in acknowledgment, then held his phone up in my face and repeated, "Can you believe this?"

I recognized the ESPN logo but couldn't quite make out the text.

"What is that?" I asked, squinting at the screen. "Is that the All-Pro list?"

"Yes!" the agitated receiver snapped. "They've got me on second team. Second team!" he shouted. "What a complete joke. These sportswriters are idiots."

Wickie had played extremely well—there was no doubt about that. He was definitely one of the league's top receivers. But this had been a big year for wideouts in general. In fact, I could think of three, possibly even four receivers who'd had better seasons overall—*and* their teams had made the playoffs. But given his current temper, I decided to keep my opinion to myself.

"Man, I led the league in catches!" Wickie continued, staring angrily at his phone. "One hundred and ten! Over twelve hundred yards! Seven touchdowns! And I finish *third* in the voting?"

Gym shook his head in sympathy. I could tell he was a little embarrassed by Wickie's outburst but was reluctant to get into a shouting match with the face of the franchise—especially in front of an outsider.

Wickie turned toward me. "You're a media guy, Coach. What were you guys thinking?"

I held my hands out in mock surrender. "Hey, I don't get to vote on this. I'm sure it was close, though. Who were the two ahead of you?"

Wickie rattled off players from Atlanta and Denver. Sure enough, they were the same guys I would have chosen.

"Well, they did have really good seasons," I pointed out.

"Sure. But neither of them had over one hundred catches. And two of Shelton's touchdowns were on punt returns! Punt returns!" He stared at me incredulously.

"But Shelton reached the NFC Championship Game. And

both of those guys made the playoffs. Maybe that's what the voters were thinking," I offered. "It *is* a team game."

Wickie closed his eyes, a pained expression sweeping across his face. "Making All-Pro is an individual award. The team has nothing to do with it!"

Huh . . . that's a bold statement, I thought. *After all, someone had to throw him the ball.*

"I did everything I could. Caught every ball. Fought for extra yards. Scored seven touchdowns," he said, ticking each item off on his fingers. "So we didn't make the playoffs. That's not *my* fault."

And with that, he spun around and disappeared back down the hall, his voice echoing in the distance. "Shelton? Are you kidding me?"

"Sorry about that, Tony," Gym apologized. "He gets a little . . . *excitable* sometimes."

I was about to tell him not to worry about it when a thought occurred to me. "Do you think he'll put two and two together as to why I'm here?"

Gym just scoffed. "Are you kidding me? Knowing that guy, he's already forgotten he even talked to us. First wide receiver I've ever known to actively petition the league to wear number 1. Had a royal fit when they told him no."

I grinned. "I'll bet he did."

"Would you like to see the concessions area?" Gym asked, shifting the mood in a more positive direction.

"I'd love to."

We had barely taken ten steps when Terry appeared around the corner and flagged us down.

"Tony! Great news," he said, beaming. "I think I've found an office for you."

Gym looked over at me and smiled. "Now this I gotta see."

SUPPLIES AND DEMANDS

"WELL . . . WHAT DO YOU THINK?" Terry looked at me, waiting for my reaction. Gym and I glanced at each other and then at the door in front of us. A small faux-wood sign with my name stamped into it had been loosely mounted above an affixed, gold-embossed placard that read "Supplies."

"You're putting him in the supply closet?" Gym asked.

"I'm afraid it's all we've got," Terry offered apologetically.

Gym opened the door, revealing a small, dimly lit room with a desk in the center. Wall-mounted shelves were loaded with toner cartridges, three-ring binders, legal pads, pens, and miscellaneous office supplies, and boxes of printer paper were stacked in the far corner.

"We're changing out the sign," Terry explained. "And we're looking for a spot to store all of this," he added, gesturing around the room.

"Don't worry about that," I assured him, stepping inside. "You might as well leave it where people are used to finding it. And I can live with 'Tony Dungy: Supplies.' I remember when I had to stick my assistant head coach, Herm Edwards, in a closet in Tampa. That was the only space available."

Gym glanced at his watch. "Listen, as much as I'd like to hang around and help you two decorate, I'm afraid I've got to run. We've got a free agency meeting starting in a few minutes." He looked up at me. "In fact, Tony, if you're up for it, you might want to sit in on that."

He was right—I did want to be there. I didn't necessarily need to understand every aspect of the team's roster decisions, but I *did* want to get a better understanding of how and why they were making them.

"Actually, I would love that," I said, making good use of my office by grabbing a yellow pad and pen from the shelf. "Terry, seriously—this setup is perfect. I wouldn't change a thing," I added as I followed Gym out into the hall.

"At least you're not outside under a tarp," Gym said as we walked away.

I laughed. "Listen, far greater men have started off with less."

•　　•　　•　　•　　•

A few minutes later, we arrived at a door marked "Personnel Meeting Room."

"Welcome to the brains behind Orlando Vipers player acquisitions," Gym announced as he opened the door.

Whiteboards filled three walls, and two large pull-down screens covered the fourth, undoubtedly where another whiteboard featured the beginning of the team's draft board for the upcoming college draft. Today would be the first preparation meeting for the approaching free agency period. Because it doesn't get as much media hoopla as the college draft does, some tend to overlook this critical component of the roster-building process. But it takes every bit as much research and preparation—sometimes even more since the financial stakes are higher.

The beauty of free agency is that it's a great way to fill holes in your roster with proven, experienced players who have solid track records in the NFL. The downside is that experience tends to come with a hefty price tag. It's like bringing in someone with a flashy résumé as opposed to hiring someone straight out of college. You know what you're getting, but you have to pay for it, and usually that means someone else in the organization will have to sacrifice. There were times in both Tampa and Indy, for example, when we brought in an above-average player or former superstar whose contract amount necessitated our releasing somebody else or renegotiating another player's contract to keep us under the salary cap.

Players in free agency who jump from team to team usually do so for a reason. When they leave their original teams, many times it is purely financial—their teams can no longer afford them. But often when a team lets a top player walk out the door, there's another explanation. And that reason sometimes becomes obvious only when the player gets to your team. So if you're not careful, a "quick fix" can lead to a lot of problems down the road. Not to mention the fact that quick fixes are typically just Band-Aids covering up larger problems. Sure, they might bring some short-term success, but great teams tend to focus more on long-term strength and stability. The way the Vipers staff evaluated their options would speak volumes about their values as an organization.

After Gym introduced me to everyone in the room, I took a seat on the periphery, while Gym settled in at the table along with Joe; Whit Jansen, the offensive coordinator; Dennis "DC" Coleman, the defensive coordinator; Stan Taylor, the special teams coordinator; and Stacy Banks, Gym's salary cap adminis-trator, or "capologist."

"The way I see it, we simply have to find a complement to Wickie on the other side," Whit began. "If I were defending us, I'd roll coverage to his side every time."

"Defenses do," Joe broke in, "especially in the red zone, which is killing us."

"Exactly," Whit concurred. "We need another threat to take the pressure off."

Gym looked skeptical. "You think Wickie will be happy if he's getting the ball *less*?"

Joe shrugged. "We'll manage. If he gets upset, we'll just promise him more touches the following week, then cross that bridge when we get there."

"So what are you proposing?" Gym asked.

Joe's eyes lit up like a Christmas tree. "Well, rumor has it Cleveland is going to release Fred Ashford this week. Now that guy's a real game changer. I think he could help us a lot!"

I looked around the table but didn't say anything. Ashford was a generational talent whose reputation for undermining coaches and stirring up trouble in the locker room was almost as prolific as his exploits on the field. If Cleveland did decide to release him, they would simply be the latest team to have been charmed by his talents, hoping things would change, only to end up with buyer's remorse by midseason.

Joe eagerly scanned the table for support. When nobody responded, he turned to Whit. "What do you think, Whit? Would Ashford fit in our offense?"

"I think he'd be a terrific fit," Whit said enthusiastically. "He'd give us a third option in the red zone along with Wickie and Don." Don Buerkle, a fifth-year running back, was another terrific talent the Vipers already had on the roster. He didn't have great hands, nor was he of much help as a blocker in the passing game, but he was a great downhill runner and could definitely eat up some yardage.

Joe quickly turned to Gym. "What do you think, Gym? We could open free agency with a splash, put everyone on notice, and transform our team at the same time." He was lobbying hard. And I could see why. A big-name acquisition *would* take some of the media's attention off Joe's lackluster record. But at what cost? After all, there was a reason Cleveland was willing to let Ashford go after just one season—despite his stellar numbers. I glanced over at Gym. He looked hesitant—and understandably so. From what little I'd observed, the team already had a bit of a prima donna on its hands with Wickie, and it was hard to imagine their undersized locker room being able to accommodate another massive ego. When Gym's eyes met mine, I put on my best poker face. I knew what I would do, but this wasn't my decision to make.

Gym looked over at Joe and Whit, both of whom were literally on the edges of their seats. After a brief pause, he turned to his capologist.

"Stacy, what would bringing Ashford in do to our cap?" The young woman glanced at her laptop, tapped a few keys, and nodded. "We could make it work."

At that point, DC muttered something I couldn't quite make out. Apparently Whit didn't catch it either, because he immediately snapped his head toward the defensive coordinator. "You got something to say, DC?"

DC took a deep breath before he spoke. He was looking straight at Joe, his focus as sharp as his tone.

"Only that the last thing this team needs is more money spent on offense."

Uh-oh. I'd been around long enough to know where this was headed.

"Look," DC said, leaning in, "it's no secret we're not one of the best defenses in the league. We're not even in the middle. My coaching staff are working their collective tails off, but there's no denying it—we're terrible overall talentwise. I'm surprised our opponents aren't scoring during time-outs."

Whit looked down and chuckled, which didn't exactly help the situation.

"Go ahead and laugh!" DC rose to his feet. "I'm over here trying to cobble together a defense with duct tape and Spackle, but sure . . . let's add another great player on offense! In fact, why not just blow our entire salary cap on offense!" He reached down, grabbed a folder off the table, and pulled out a sheet of paper.

"A friend of mine in Buffalo got his capologist to run an analysis of our spending for me," he announced holding the sheet up. Stacy narrowed her eyes, clearly upset that DC had gone around her. I couldn't say that I blamed her. Sharing information—confidential or not—with people outside the team is pretty bad form. I glanced over at Joe, fully expecting him to explode, but his eyes were fixed on the sheet DC was holding in front of him. I couldn't make out any specifics, just a large yellow-and-blue pie chart.

"See the yellow?" DC asked, pointing to the chart. "That's what we spend on offense. And the blue is defense." He turned the sheet toward himself and studied it. "Look at this thing! It looks like Pac-Man! The yellow is devouring the blue! That's the way it's always been here. Offense consumes defense." He stared defiantly at Gym, who seemed to be at a complete loss for words. For the moment, everyone seemed to have forgotten that I was in the room, and I had to admit I was grateful.

Stan just sat quietly at the far end of the table. The Vipers special teams unit was actually fairly functional. I'm sure there were a handful of players Stan would love to lobby for, but given that special teams was often overlooked, speaking up at this point would not only be futile but possibly a little dangerous.

After taking a deep breath, Whit turned to Gym and barked, "Look, we had fourth-quarter leads in four losses last year. We did our job. If they could hold a lead," he pointed at DC, "and we had won just *one* of those games, we'd have been in the playoffs. Two of them and we would have won the division— maybe even had a home playoff game. But *no*. The defense lost all four leads. And not to the Drew Breeses or Tom Bradys of the league either."

DC's face was crimson. I kept waiting for Joe to rein in this conversation. When he finally leaned forward, I breathed a quiet sigh of relief.

"Listen, I agree our defense has to improve." Joe's voice was loud enough to take control of the moment. "But until they do, we have to be able to outscore our opponents. We need to put as many points on the board as we can—as fast as we can. *That's* how we'll win!"

Okay . . . maybe not where I would've gone.

DC threw up his hands. "That's the other thing. Our offense is constantly throwing the ball and running no-huddle and up-tempo. I like it when we score—I really do—but Whit, *your* offense acts like it's at a track meet, going up and down the field as fast as possible. That means my defense—most of whom are north of thirty, low draft picks, or guys *he* was able to get cheap when they were cut from other teams," he said, pointing at Gym, "are back out on the field almost immediately! And now you're adding *another* wide receiver?"

At that point, Gym piped in. "Hold on a second, DC. Nobody's committed to anything yet." But DC just kept going.

"And why?" he asked, raising his voice and gesturing dismissively at Whit. "Because all *this* guy cares about is getting his own head coaching gig someday. Every game is just one more audition tape—one more chance for him to show the football world what an offensive genius he is!"

Now *that* got Whit out of his seat.

"Wait just a minute," Whit sputtered, staring DC down. But before he could finish, Joe was up, arms spread out like a ref in a title fight, keeping the two men apart.

"All right, everybody take it easy!" Gym said, bringing the moment to a halt. "Clearly we've got issues that need to be addressed on both sides of the ball."

And in this room.

"I've got the scouting reports on Ashford," Gym continued, his voice low and calm. "And Stacy, if you could please run me the numbers . . ." She nodded and shot DC a defiant glare.

"I'll review everything, make a few calls of my own, and get back to you all with my decision," Gym said.

Then he turned to me, drawing the attention of Joe, Whit, and DC—all of whom blushed in sudden realization of everything that had just unfolded. "Tony," he said with an apologetic smile, "welcome to the Vipers."

DODGEBALL

ALMOST TWO WEEKS HAD PASSED since the free agency blowup. Despite Joe's and Gym's best efforts to reconcile matters between the dueling coordinators, tensions were still high around the team's offices—in part because Gym had held off so long on making a decision that Fred Ashford ended up signing with Miami without the Vipers making an offer. Frankly, I thought we'd dodged a bullet, but Joe and Whit were furious.

At first, it had looked like Ashford's asking price was going to be too high for the Vipers to consider anyway, but as the days passed with no takers, his agent began to realize there wasn't much of a market for an aging receiver who had been suspended multiple times for insubordination and behavioral issues and unceremoniously released by four teams over the course of his career. Finally, after a week on the market, Ashford's agent called Gym and proposed a four-year contract with a midlevel signing bonus and a first-year salary at the league minimum, with small increases set for each of the following three years. Very team friendly.

In Joe's mind, it was a no-brainer. After all, the Vipers could clearly afford the contract, and Ashford *was* a tremendous talent.

But Gym wasn't convinced Ashford was worth it—even at a discount. Wickie was already providing more than enough "excitement" in the locker room, and the thought of adding Ashford into the mix was tough to picture.

Still, Joe was certain he could handle the personalities, so after his arguments to Gym fell on deaf ears, he went over Gym's head to Terry to plead his case. As they were meeting, Ashford signed with Miami, making it a moot issue. But Joe was still upset and blamed Gym for the whole thing.

"He hasn't spoken to me since Ashford signed," Gym said during one of our informal afternoon meetings. "Not that we've had much time to speak, with the draft coming up and all. Still, he's gone out of his way to make it clear that he's displeased." Gym glanced around my makeshift office, now decorated with pictures of Lauren and the kids, as well as some crayon drawings from my youngest, Jaela. "By the way, I like what you've done with the place."

"Thanks," I agreed, looking around. "I think it has a certain understated charm." He smiled, but I could tell he was second-guessing himself about Ashford. "Listen, Gym, for what it's worth, I think your reasoning on not offering Ashford a contract was sound."

Gym nodded. "Thanks. I get Joe's reasoning, too, though. He's *got* to win this season. Of course, so do I," he continued. "But like most coaches, he thinks more in the short term than a GM. And he should. I get it."

"But this would've been a bad signing, even in the short term," I reassured him. "Just ask Cleveland, or Houston, or San Diego, or . . ."

Gym smiled and waved me off. "Okay, I get it. Still, all that hullabaloo two weeks ago was for nothing."

"I wouldn't say that," I countered. "It definitely brought some important issues to the surface."

"Like our lack of a solid defense?" He sighed.

"No. I meant the frustrations between Whit and DC, and Joe siding with his offensive coordinator."

"And now Joe's not talking to me," he added, the frustration coming through in his tone. I'd known him only socially, but Gym had never struck me as being hung up on title or position. Still, it was clear that Joe's taking his concerns up the ladder to Terry had really upset him. I leaned back in my chair. I definitely hadn't missed this side of the business. When things are going well, everyone gets along beautifully. But when they're not, things can get ugly in a hurry. Not only were the two coordinators avoiding talking to each other, but now the head coach also wasn't talking to the GM—and the college draft was just around the corner.

This was going to be interesting.

•　　•　　•　　•　　•

"I think we're all here," Gym announced, bringing conversation in the room to a stop, "so why don't we go ahead and get started."

The room was packed. Joe, Whit, DC, Stan, Scott Pendleton, who was the director of college scouting, and a number of other team scouts were seated around the main table. The individual position coaches lined the sides of the room. Not wanting to get in the way, I took a seat in the corner next to Wilson Grady, the wide receivers coach. All around the room, whiteboards labeled RANK BY POSITION were filled with neat rows of colorful magnets denoting players the scouts had been watching, while another board, labeled OVERALL, sat empty. Gym clicked his remote, and a large white screen began to lower from the ceiling behind him. "Scott," he said, handing the remote to the Vipers' young scouting director, "it's all yours."

"Thanks, Gym."

Seeing Gym take a seat next to Joe, I thought, *Well, that's a step in the right direction.*

Scott clicked the remote, and the headshot and stats for Anthony Jobe from UCLA filled the screen.

"First up is Jobe, a senior running back," Scott began. "He could've put his name in the draft last year but didn't, which was smart, because this was far and away his best season. He's six one, 220, very productive in the passing game, and hard to bring down. He also has a great change of direction and gets a lot of yards after contact.

"Medically, he's a B," Scott continued. "He had a knee injury his freshman year and missed six games. He's probably an end-of-the-first-round guy and might slip to the second. I give him a 6.2 plus."

I craned my neck toward the board behind me and saw that Jobe was the third magnet under the RB column. The 6.2 rating put him in the highest tier of running backs, just behind a junior from Boston College. The "plus" meant that he fit the Vipers' scheme with respect to his skills. In other words, the best running back fit for their offense was one who could also catch a couple of short passes every game. Some players might be extremely effective in certain aspects of the game, but that doesn't necessarily mean they fit with a team's system. A running quarterback, for example, might not be the best fit for a team looking for a precision passer. Likewise, a big, space-filling defensive tackle might not be the best choice for a defense trying to build a quick and agile line.

Denny Green used to say, "The fifty-three best players don't make the best team," and he was absolutely right. The whole unit has to function well together, or else even the most talented players won't be able to perform to the best of their abilities.

After Scott finished his assessment, one of the two national scouts spoke up. "I watched him practice at UCLA as well. His practice habits are okay, but he's not great in the weight room, so there's definitely room for improvement."

As the regional scout assigned to the West Coast added his two cents to the discussion, Wilson leaned over to me and murmured, "He may be a great running back, but characterwise, Jobe is an F minus. Not a good kid."

"Bad work habits, or off-field?" I asked.

"Mostly work habits," he whispered, "though he's been arrested a few times for bar fights. I've known their strength coach for years, and he told me he can't wait for that kid to be gone. Says he's not much on the practice field either—that he tends to zone out on plays when he doesn't get the ball."

"What about the classroom?"

Wilson grimaced. "My buddy says he has no idea how he's even still eligible."

"Well . . . UCLA *is* a tough school," I conceded.

"Yeah, but apparently Jobe has zero interest in his classes—zero," he added, forming his index finger and thumb into a 0.

As Wilson settled back into his chair, I turned my attention to the regional scout. What Wilson said likely had credence. More often than not, strength coaches are the best sources for background information on different players. Not only do they interact with the players most frequently—often daily, both in season and out—but their interactions also take place away from all the bright lights, TV cameras, and crowds, so they typically see and hear things most people don't.

Odds are, both the regional and national scouts—as well as Scott—would have spoken to the strength coach, so I was surprised when none of them mentioned any of these issues.

I leaned over to Wilson. "Are you going to say anything?"

Without breaking eye contact with the screen, he shrugged and replied, "Not my problem."

Wow. It didn't surprise me to see the offensive and defensive coordinators at each other's throats, but one offensive position coach holding out information that might help the team? Now *that* was a first.

After the regional scout finished his comments, Scott clicked the remote, pulling up the next Bruin—this time, a wide receiver. Wilson leaned forward in his seat.

"Here we go," he said, his eyes lighting up. "Now *this* guy could be interesting."

I stayed for the rest of the UCLA, USC, and San Diego State presentations, and I couldn't help but notice that neither the scouts nor the coaches ever openly addressed any character-related issues—good or bad—when they discussed their target players. As the discussion shifted over to Stanford, I jotted a few quick notes and quietly slipped out of the room.

•   •   •   •   •

During the next several weeks, the OVERALL board began to fill up as the coaches and scouts continued to assess players. Anthony Jobe was one of several top running backs flown in, even though the team had little interest in using their first-round pick on a back because Don Buerkle was still in the prime of his career. But since all predraft visits must be reported to the NFL and are then made available to the other clubs, the Vipers—like most teams—used a number of their visits as smoke screens for their real interests and intentions.

Interestingly, the team didn't fly in any tight ends, even though that position had become the focus of its first pick. While the move disguised their interest and probably did throw their competition off the scent, I had always preferred to meet face-to-face with the players I was going to make a major investment in. Then I could see how they handled themselves in a professional setting and make sure they were a good fit, personalitywise, for the program. I'd said as much to Joe and Gym, but in the end, they believed their brief interviews at the Scouting Combine had been sufficient to get to know the players.

Time would tell.

By the end of April, the draft was upon us. Jobe ended up being selected by Baltimore as the penultimate pick of the first round, while the Vipers opted to use their first-round pick on a promising tight end out of the University of Minnesota.

In addition to the tight end, I was intrigued by their sixth-round pick, Wesley Robinson. Wesley was a raw wide receiver out of Carson-Newman, a small school in the hills of Tennessee, just outside Knoxville. I'd been in the office the day the Vipers flew him in and was incredibly impressed with his maturity.

When all was said and done, most of the national and local sports scribes yawned at the team's draft, giving the team Bs and B minuses across the board. I was holding off on my assessment until I got a chance to meet and observe the incoming rookie class at minicamp the following month. It would be my first opportunity to see the full Vipers roster in action—the one remaining thing I wanted to do before making my recommendations to Terry.

ONE FOR THE DOGS

THE START OF MINICAMP has always been one of my favorite days of the year. The promise of a new season and the optimism of youth emanate through the building and across the practice fields, making it a perfect bookend to the dreaded final cuts of training camp.

It's the first time that new players acquired through free agency and the college draft get a chance to play and work out with the returning players. The hope is that veterans will set the standard for young guys, that each rookie will put his best foot forward, and that everyone will get along and complement each other well. Of course, with jobs at stake and some players looking over their shoulders at newcomers, the possibility exists that things won't go smoothly.

As I came out onto the field, I saw the first team, including Wickie, on the field running plays. I stood next to Wesley Robinson, the newly acquired rookie wide receiver, who was talking on the sideline to his position coach, Wilson Grady. Compared to Joe and Whit, Wilson was a relatively young

THE SOUL OF A TEAM

coach who'd been in the NFL for only two seasons, yet Wesley appeared to be locked into every word he was saying.

It was a hot day, even for Florida in April, and the players were in helmets, jerseys, and shorts but no pads, with offensive players wearing white jerseys with black numbers and green trim and defensive players in black jerseys with green numbers and white trim. The quarterbacks all had lime-green tanks over their jerseys. Personally, I'd always liked the simplicity of the Colts' blue and white, but it was no surprise that gear showcasing the Vipers' sharp color combination had risen to the top of the NFL in sales. My kids loved it—especially Justin. Ever since the team had come to Orlando three years earlier, Lauren and I had struggled to get him to wear *anything* that didn't have the Vipers logo on it. I knew he'd be devastated if the team moved to Oakland. Hopefully, this new roster would help turn things around.

Once Wilson finished giving his last set of instructions, Wesley sprinted off the sideline toward the huddle, tapping Wickie on the shoulder to come out. Wickie pivoted, glanced back at the rookie as Wesley entered the huddle, then slowly made his way to the sideline. He hadn't even cleared the field yet when the ball was snapped.

"Come on, Wickie," Wilson shouted as the veteran wide receiver strolled toward the sideline. "Hustle it up!"

Wickie kept his head down as he made his way over to the bench, then lifted his helmet and took a drink from one of the Gatorade bottles littering the sideline. Back on the field, Brendan Quinlan, the backup quarterback, ran a bootleg to the side opposite from where Wesley was lined up, and the rookie receiver dashed in front of the cornerback and positioned himself as if to block. Actual blocking would wait until the team practiced with pads. I watched as Wesley continued to run plays with the second team, sprinting in and out of the huddle, occasionally taking a few steps toward Wilson to receive instruction.

"Wesley looks pretty good," I said, coming up alongside Wilson.

"He does," he responded, then motioned for the slot receiver to take a step back off the line of scrimmage.

"Farther!" he called out. "One more step back, Zach!" The offending receiver dutifully obeyed. When the ball was snapped, Wesley streaked out of his stance on the outside, beating the defensive back off the ball and racing—alone and wide open—down the field. A whistle sounded, stopping the play, and I looked back and saw that Brendan had been "sacked," which in a no-tackle drill basically means he had been touched by a defensive lineman.

As Wesley ran back toward the huddle, Wilson motioned him over and sent in another receiver to take his place.

"Didn't you hear the audible?" Wilson asked.

Wesley put both hands on his helmet in regret. "I'm sorry, Coach," he apologized. "I completely forgot."

"Don't worry," Wilson assured him, slapping the young receiver on the shoulder. "You'll get it."

"Yes, sir," Wesley responded, taking a knee next to Wilson to watch the next play.

"I'm afraid I missed it too," I confessed.

Wilson smiled and explained, "The cornerback was cheating toward the quarterback, so Brendan called 'Utah' before the snap, which is our alert read for a blitz. Wesley's got to learn to adjust his route to a quick slant off the line. He's a sharp kid. He'll get it."

I nodded. The leap from college to the pros is bigger than most people think. Rookies have to take in a lot all at once— new schemes, new plays, new coverages, new routes—and everything comes at them much faster than they're used to. That's why I always looked at prospects' academic records leading up to the draft. Raw talent is great, but the best players are almost always students of the game as well. Peyton Manning, for example, was one of the most cerebral quarterbacks I'd ever seen. He had a great arm and pinpoint accuracy, but it was his mental aptitude and understanding of the game that always gave us an extra edge.

"You've got to love Wesley's energy, though," Wilson continued. "Even his mistakes are at full tilt. He was a good forty yards out of position by the time the whistle blew!"

"Attitude and effort," I replied, nodding. "That's the magic combination."

Brendan ran a few more plays before the first team went back in to take the final eight snaps. Wickie and Don loafed, sleepwalking through most of the plays. Don missed two blocks, both resulting in "sacks" to the starting quarterback, Austin Quarles. And though Wickie and Austin were able to connect on two passes, Austin had to make some pretty obvious adjustments to hit the slow-trotting receiver in stride. Likewise, I couldn't help but notice the opposing defensive back deliberately slowing his pace so the pass could be completed without contact. It was hard to imagine our star players on the Colts— Peyton Manning, Marvin Harrison, Reggie Wayne, or Edgerrin James—just going through the motions the way these guys did. It wasn't even that our Colts coaching staff had demanded full-speed practices; they were just wired that way. It was their nature to go all out, all the time.

Sure, this was just a padless minicamp scrimmage, but how were Whit and the other offensive coaches supposed to effectively evaluate which plays would work in an actual game if half the offensive players were running at half speed? And it wasn't just the offense. While some rushers were coming hard off the ball, others were practically standing still on the line, which meant many of the offensive linemen and running backs weren't getting much out of the practice either. Frankly, it was a little hard to watch. It was even harder to see the rookies on the sideline watching the veterans—the guys who were supposed to set the example for how to practice—dog it.

Maybe it would all straighten itself out once they put on pads, but somehow I doubted it. Details matter.

I'd seen everything I needed to see.

PRESIDENTIAL REPORT

THE FOLLOWING MONDAY, I met Terry in his office. He looked tired.

"Late night?" I asked.

"You could say that," he said, pushing a copy of the *Orlando Press* across his desk.

"People still get actual newspapers?" I replied, turning the paper around to face me.

"Let's hope not," Terry stated, his expression flat.

One glance at the headline told me everything I needed to know: "Vipers Owner Talking Possible Oakland Move."

Wow. No wonder Terry looked exhausted. "When did this break?" I asked.

"Late yesterday afternoon." Terry sighed. "Someone at the *Press* overheard Owen talking with one of his West Coast contacts over lunch." He closed his eyes and began rubbing his temples. "Less than three months before the start of the season and eight months before the stadium referendum vote."

"Well, that's not good," I said, verbalizing the obvious.

"No, it's not. I've had four Orlando city commissioners call me already, and just before you came in, the governor of Florida called. He said, and I quote, 'Don't let the door hit you on your way out.'"

Ouch. "I'm so sorry, Terry."

"He also said he'd veto any attempt at state funding for a new stadium."

I looked at the notebook in my hand. Maybe now wasn't the best time to give him my evaluation of the organization. I was about to suggest we move our meeting to another day when Terry noticed the notebook. His eyes met mine and a half-hearted smile crossed his lips.

"I don't suppose you've got any good news for me?"

At least he hadn't lost his sense of humor.

"I don't know if it's good," I laughed, "but it's definitely timely."

"That's good enough for me." He took a deep breath and sat up in his chair. "Let's hear it."

●   ●   ●   ●   ●

"Okay." I riffled through my notes, very much aware that I was speaking to a former federal judge—and a tired, frustrated one at that. "Well, let me start by reiterating that you've got some fantastic people in this organization, Terry. A lot of good, solid talent, on and off the field."

He raised his eyebrows. "But . . ."

"Let's not get there too fast. Having talent is important." I paused. "But I *have* seen some things over the past few weeks that concern me."

"Such as?"

"Well," I said, nodding at the newspaper sitting on the desk between us, "for starters . . ."

"There's Owen." Terry sighed in frustration.

"Yes, Owen. Now don't be too hard on him," I cautioned. "Owen's basically a good guy. And he really does love this city. But right now, Owen's one and only goal is to win the Super Bowl."

"And get a shiny new stadium," Terry added.

"*And* get a shiny new stadium," I agreed.

"I'm still not sure I understand what the problem is," Terry confessed. "I mean, look around." He gestured around his cramped and poorly lit office. "We *do* need a bigger, better facility and stadium. And who *doesn't* want to win the Super Bowl?"

"But at what cost?" I asked.

That set him back on his heels a little.

"What do you mean?"

"Look at what he's willing to do to get there—turn over the entire coaching staff, move the team, alienate the fan base, abandon the community . . ." I set my notebook on his desk and leaned in to plead my case. "Look, the fact that Owen is already thinking about moving the team after only three years shows where his priorities lie. And as the owner, he sets the tone for the entire organization. His values are reflected in everyone else—"

"Now wait a minute," Terry interjected. "I never endorsed moving the team out of Orlando."

"No, but you *were* thinking about firing Gym and Joe. Where did that come from?"

A wave of realization washed over his face.

"Terry, there's nothing wrong with wanting to win, or holding people accountable," I assured him. "But the way you go about it speaks volumes about your organization. Look at Joe and Whit. They were willing to completely overlook all of Fred Ashford's red flags because of what he can do on the field. Sure, he might win you another game or two, but is that really the kind of guy you want on your team?"

"But we ended up not taking Ashford," Terry reminded me.

"That's true," I conceded. "But Gym *did* sign off on several players in the draft solely on the recommendation of your scouts, and I couldn't help but notice that neither character issues nor concerns about work ethic featured very prominently, if at all, in their overall reports."

"So you're saying we've made some bad draft picks?"

"Not necessarily, but what I *am* saying is that what you invest in now will determine the kind of returns you see in the future. As college coaches say, 'You recruit your problems.' Or here, draft them."

"And you think we're investing in the wrong things," he said thoughtfully.

"To an extent . . . yes."

Terry looked frustrated. I really felt for him. The truth is, the Vipers weren't doing anything that almost every other franchise did as a matter of course. There's a reason one team after another kept signing Fred Ashford, despite his reputation. And Joe certainly wasn't the only head coach whose neck was on the chopping block this season. Unfortunately, more often than not, surface-level fixes yield only surface-level results. If you want long-term changes and solutions, you need to dig a little deeper and get at the root of the problem.

I decided to change my tactic a bit. "Look, Terry," I said, sitting back in my chair. "I've only been here for a couple of months, but from what little I've seen, I think the biggest problem you have with this team—" I paused to emphasize the point—"is that it's *not* a team."

"What do you mean, *not a team*?" Terry's voice carried a defensive edge, so I flipped through my notes again to give him a chance to breathe. By nature and training Terry was a very calm, even-tempered guy, but having to run defense that morning on Owen's slipup had raised his stress level.

"Well, look at Joe." It seemed as good a place to start as any. "The poor guy was so paranoid about losing his job that he either didn't realize his coordinators were at each other's throats or didn't care. And now that he does realize it, he keeps siding with Whit, which, of course, puts DC on the defensive. No pun intended."

"Well, Joe's career as an assistant, before he became a head coach, was all on the offensive side of the ball. So it's kind of natural that he would gravitate toward Whit's side," Terry rationalized.

"Yes, but he's the head coach now. And besides, how do you think that makes DC feel? Whit gets all the high draft picks and free agency attention, and DC's . . ."

"The odd man out," Terry finished.

"Actually," I corrected him, "that distinction probably belongs to Stan."

"Wow. I totally forgot about Stan."

"Like everyone else." Being the special teams coordinator is a tough gig. You often have to make do with everyone else's leftovers, and if there's ever a salary-cap crisis, your guys are typically the first to go. And yet every season, two or three games are decided by a long field goal, a kickoff return, or a blocked extra point, which is when people suddenly remember that you exist.

"The point is, Terry, everyone's so busy looking out for themselves and lobbying for resources for their *own* units that nobody's looking at the big picture. That's human nature, but not the path to a successful team. They aren't thinking about how they can complement each other or what would be best for everyone. They're just pointing fingers, casting blame, and looking for ways to make the system work in their favor—even if it's at the other guy's expense. That's not a team mentality."

Terry thought for a moment, then spoke. "So . . . are you saying the issue is with the coaching staff?"

"Part of it," I said. "Again, I've only been here a couple of months, but based on the tape I've watched from last season and what I saw at minicamp, you've got some problems on the field as well."

Terry sighed and sat back in his chair. "Let me guess—Wickie, right?"

I nodded. "Yeah . . . he's definitely a piece of the puzzle. He's got a lot of talent, but he also cares more about his own stats than he does about tallies in the win column."

"Yeah, but one *can* lead to the other, right?" Terry countered. "I mean, if enough guys like Wickie have breakout seasons, the whole team benefits."

I could see where he was going, though I wasn't sure I agreed. "Well . . . yes and no. Again, you're talking about a short-term fix. You can't always count on three or four guys having breakout seasons simultaneously. That's like betting your whole season on winning every coin toss. Marquee players are a great luxury to have. But the goal is to be consistently strong across the board. I'll take steady players who do the little things well all the time over a single All-Pro wideout any day of the week. If the offensive line doesn't give Austin enough time to throw the ball downfield, it doesn't matter how fast Wickie is."

Terry nodded in agreement. "Okay, I see your point."

"The really frustrating piece, though, is that Wickie could be a great role model for the rookies. A guy with his talent could and should raise the bar for everyone else—make the whole team better. But the way he was dogging it at minicamp and giving Wesley the cold shoulder was kind of hard to watch."

"Well," Terry hedged, "most wide receivers have some issues."

"It's not just Wickie, though," I pointed out. "If you watch the film, you'll see that Don tends to pull up on his blocks on plays where he doesn't get the ball. Austin had to pick himself up off the ground about a dozen times last season because Don wasn't doing his job—including the hit he took against Cincinnati that knocked him out of the game."

Terry frowned. "Not only out of that game; it also landed Austin on the sideline for two weeks. Probably cost us a playoff spot."

I nodded. "Possibly. And Wickie and Don are not the only ones. I saw a lot of guys on film—solid veterans—dropping coverages, not hustling, missing tackles, not securing the ball, walking to the line when the tempo needed to be quick. It all adds up."

"And don't forget the penalties," Terry added. "We were one of the most penalized teams in the league last year. Offensive holding, lining up offside, defensive holding, blocks in the back . . ."

"Penalties are usually a sign of a lack of discipline," I said. "Drives coaches crazy."

"And loses games," Terry tacked on.

"*And* loses games."

He was starting to get the picture—infighting among the staff; some guys playing only for themselves, others not doing their jobs; and a decided lack of positive core values guiding their decisions and moving them forward. "So," Terry said, letting out a deep breath, "got any ideas on how to fix all of this?"

"Well, whether or not you can fix everything is up to you guys, but I do have a few ideas I think will help."

"Such as?" He leaned forward and slid a pad in front of him, ready to take notes.

We spent the next few hours discussing what I'd noticed on the field and in meetings, as well as what I'd heard from the coaches and players who'd stopped by my office.

Finally Terry said, "You've given me plenty to think about, Tony. What do you recommend as a first step?"

"How about bringing everyone together to talk more about this?" I suggested.

He nodded and declared, "Consider it done."

THE DIAGNOSIS

A FEW DAYS AFTER TERRY AND I MET, the entire Vipers coaching staff assembled in the main conference room after receiving a cryptic e-mail from Terry. He'd said only that "there will be a mandatory meeting in the main conference room tomorrow morning at 9:00 to discuss the future of the Vipers organization," which resulted in an apprehensive atmosphere.

As the last of the position coaches filed into the room, Terry rose from his seat. "I think we're all here," he began, "with the exception of Owen. He asked me to relay his apologies. He had to fly out west for a last-minute business meeting."

A murmur filled the room. Terry had worked the phones nonstop over the past forty-eight hours to calm the media storm after Owen's proposed plan to move the franchise to Oakland was leaked, and thanks to an unusually busy news cycle, most of the larger outlets had moved on to other things. Clearly, however, the rest of the Vipers organization had not.

"As you know, I asked Coach Dungy to spend a little time observing our organization this off-season to see if he could shed light on why we seem to be struggling to break out as a team." A few muted rumblings came from the back of the room, but a quick glance from Terry brought them to a halt.

"Tony and I met on Monday," he continued, "and he shared his initial thoughts with me. He's asked to share them with you this morning." The room was dead silent, the air damp with trepidation. Then he turned to me. "Tony?"

"Thanks, Terry."

I opted to remain seated since I wanted to keep this as non-confrontational as possible. I needed to keep the focus on principles, not personalities. It was one thing to be pointed and blunt in my private analysis for Terry, but this situation needed to be handled more delicately.

"As Terry said, I've spent the past couple of months getting to know you a little better, both as individuals and as a team. I've sat in on meetings, met with most of you one-on-one, observed the mandatory minicamp, and watched *a lot* of game film. I have to say, I'm really impressed with you all. You do many things well. *Very* well.

"The fact that you've been on the verge of making the playoffs for three straight years is fantastic for any franchise, let alone one as new as yours. In fact, there are a number of other teams in this league that would love to have the record you've got." I was trying my best to ease the tension in the room, but the sea of crossed arms and skeptical expressions facing me all but shouted, *Just get on with it already!*

"Of course, that's not to say there isn't room for improvement," I continued.

"You're not going to make us do a trust fall or a ropes course, are you?" someone said from the back of the room, triggering a chorus of laughter.

"No." I joined in the laughter, grateful that someone had finally broken the ice.

"But you *do* think the problem revolves around teamwork," Terry interjected, bringing us back on track.

"Yes, I do," I replied, then turned back to the group. "I told Terry I think the Vipers are missing something—something that, in my experience, all successful, high-functioning teams have." I stood up and walked over to the only whiteboard in the room that wasn't covered in *X*s and *O*s. "What this team is missing," I said, pulling the cap off a dry-erase marker, "is a soul."

Confused faces stared back at me. Even Terry looked a little dubious.

"A *what*?" DC asked.

"A soul," I said, writing the word *SOUL* in all caps.

There was a moment's pause; then Gym spoke up. "Okay, I'll bite. What's the 'SOUL' of a team?"

"SOUL," I explained, "is an acronym that represents four essential principles practiced by truly effective teams. In fact, in all my years of coaching and working with other team leaders—not only in this league but also in professional basketball, baseball, and hockey, in sports at the college level, and even with corporate executives—I've yet to encounter a successful team that doesn't practice these principles."

"Sounds easy enough," said Whit. "What are they?"

"Now hold up there, Whit," I said, smiling. "If it were easy, every team would be operating at peak efficiency. You have to commit yourself to it, work at it—and everybody in the organization has to be on board. As I told Terry—and Owen—great teams don't just happen overnight."

"So . . ." Stan piped in, "what do we have to do?" I noticed he had a legal pad on his lap and was already taking notes; a handful of others around him noticed as well and began fumbling for their laptops. Soon the rest of the room was following suit. I shot a quick glance at Terry, who gave me a nod of encouragement.

"The *S*," I began, "stands for *selflessness*—putting your own individual goals aside for the sake of the team."

"That one's got Wickie's name written all over it," joked Wilson, prompting snickers from several others in the room.

"Listen," I said, regaining control of the conversation, "I'm sure we could all name about a dozen players—and coaches—who don't fit this description. But what I want to focus on today is what it looks like when you get it right.

"I remember one time in Indianapolis when we were playing the Green Bay Packers. They had a blitzing defense, and Tom Moore, our offensive coordinator, came to me early in the week and said, 'If this team is going to blitz on every play and leave our receivers one-on-one against their defensive backs, I say we throw on every down until they stop.' And when we went into the game, that's exactly what we did. We threw twenty-two straight passes."

That got a chuckle from Whit.

"Now, Edgerrin James was our All-Pro running back, and all he did for the first quarter and a half was block blitzing line-backers. After it was all over, he told me it wasn't a fun game for him. It certainly didn't help his stats, but he never complained. He never went over to Tom and said, 'We gotta run it; give me the ball.' He just blocked for twenty-two straight plays. A lot of people wouldn't have done that, but that's how you win. That's what being a *selfless* player looks like." Heads nodded in agreement around the table. Then Joe spoke up.

"Yeah . . . but how do you get a guy to act like that?"

"That's the challenge. Part of the *how* and *why* will become clear when we reach the *L* in SOUL.

"But for one thing, you look to bring in the right kind of

player to begin with. Our draft boards in Tampa and Indianapolis had a special section we labeled DNDC—Do Not Draft because of Character. We filled it in as we heard the scouting reports so we wouldn't be tempted to go after the wrong kind of players on draft day. And believe me, that portion of the boards always contained the names of some very talented players. You always think about making an exception to your standard in order to gain a super-talented guy, so that's why we created the category. Once we determined that a player didn't fit our character model, *we would not take him*, no matter how good he was on the field.

"It *can* be tempting," I confessed. "But when push comes to shove, you have to ask yourself, *Are we who we say we are? Or are we going to make an exception?*" I glanced around the room. "Good teams—teams with SOUL—don't make that kind of exception."

I sensed the tension rising again, so I shifted the conversation a bit.

"You also encourage selflessness by praising it when it happens. If you consistently send the message that putting the team first is a high value, eventually the players will come on board."

"Or leave and seek their glory elsewhere," warned Joe. Several others nodded and whispered among themselves.

"Yes," I conceded, "that's definitely a risk. But if they're not in agreement with what you're trying to do as a team, you have to ask yourself, *Are they really helping us anyway?*"

A couple of the coaches shook their heads in disagreement as the room went quiet.

I told them it wouldn't be easy.

•　　•　　•　　•　　•

"So you get the basic idea on selflessness. Now, *O* stands for *ownership*." Terry and Gym exchanged concerned glances. "And no," I reassured them, "I'm not talking about the owner of the team." Muffled laughter filled the room.

"What I *am* talking about is owning your *role*. This is something Coach Noll drilled into us all the time: 'Everyone's role is significant. No matter what you do, you're an important part of this team, so you have to know your job backward and forward and do your job with100 percent effort all the time.'"

"You mean we shouldn't have guys who quit on plays, or just mail it in when they aren't getting the ball," offered one of the assistant coaches.

"Or defensive guys who dog it on punt returns because they don't want to get hurt on a special teams play," Stan chimed in.

"Yes, that's part of it," I said. And it was. But I really wanted them to start thinking in terms of what the correct behavior looks like. I glanced down at my notes and saw a name I expected most of them would be hearing for the first time. "Let me give you an idea of what I'm talking about. The year the Colts won the Super Bowl, we had an offensive lineman named Charlie Johnson." Their confused expressions confirmed my original suspicion— even now, almost no one knew who Charlie was.

"He was a tight end at Oklahoma State and was athletic, but not quite fast enough to be a tight end at the pro level. We drafted him and switched him to offensive tackle, and he spent his entire rookie year just learning the position. He worked his tail off every day at practice, did his film studies, listened to his coaches, and put in his time in the weight room. During seventeen games, he played very little. Most of that was mop-up time if we were way ahead. Then in the second quarter of the Super Bowl, Ryan Diem, our starting right tackle, got his leg rolled up, so Charlie had to go in and play the rest of the game against Adewale Ogunleye, Chicago's best defensive lineman." I paused. They knew who Ogunleye was.

"I'm not kidding you—based on Charlie's performance, no one even knew Ryan was on the sideline. Charlie kept Ogunleye in check that entire game. And to this day, most people don't know he was even in there. That's what owning your role looks like."

"That's a great story, Tony," said Joe. I couldn't tell if he was being sarcastic. "But again, how do you get guys to do that? Isn't Charlie the exception?"

I was pleased. Joe really seemed to be genuine in asking this question and open to learning about another way.

"I don't think he has to be. Joe, I'm not telling you anything you haven't already done for years." I meant that, but it appeared as though he might have forgotten it of late. "You start by holding them accountable—especially the veterans."

My mind flashed back to the minicamp scrimmage when the coaches chewed out Wesley for missing a blitz but then let Don's half-hearted attempt at a block slide.

"Rookies mimic what they see. Your job is to make sure they're seeing the right things and calling it out when they don't. That," I added, "is what it looks like when coaches own their roles. A mistake is a mistake no matter who makes it. If it's a correctable error for a rookie, it's a correctable error for everyone."

I noticed a few of the position coaches shifting uncomfortably in their chairs. They were starting to grasp that the principles of SOUL applied to them as well, and the next letter was sure to get their attention.

●   ●   ●   ●   ●

"That brings us to *U*, for *unity*. Bottom line, this is a team sport, and if you're going to have any chance of winning, everyone's got to be on the same page, following the same philosophy, and working toward the same goals." Heads nodded all around the room.

"A few years ago, I was talking with Bruce Bowen. Some of you may remember Bruce, who played for the San Antonio Spurs and won a bunch of championships with them. But before he found his niche with the Spurs, he was a journeyman who played for a lot of basketball teams—and for several Hall of Fame coaches. When I asked him who was the best coach he ever played for, he answered, 'Gregg Popovich, because he had something that none of my other coaches had.'"

I noticed Joe sit a little straighter in his chair, listening intently. "Bruce told me that Gregg's star players, Tim Duncan and David Robinson, were both totally sold out to him and his philosophy. When Gregg said, 'This is how we do things here,' David and Tim completely adopted his approach too, and everybody else fell in line. Bruce told me he had other coaches who said, 'This is how we're doing it,' and their star players told them, 'Hey, Coach, do what you want, but I'm doing it my way.' So the coaches were handcuffed.

"When I took over with the Bucs, the first thing I did was sit down with Warren Sapp and say, 'Hey, Warren, if we're going to win a championship, I need you to get on board with what I'm trying to do, because people are going to follow you. And if they're following you in our direction, we're going to be a championship team. But if they're following you in a different direction—away from where we want to go—it's going to hold us back.' Fortunately, Warren did get on board, and eventually, everyone else followed."

"Yeah . . . but what if *your* unit *doesn't* have a star player?" DC grumbled, drawing an angry glare from Whit and an eye roll from Joe. Strangely enough, I'd actually been hoping this might come up.

"I'm glad you asked that, DC, because what I'm talking about starts right here in this room." I paused for a second to make sure I had everyone's attention.

"Most people think, *If I could just get better players, our team would be better.* But that's erroneous thinking. The goal is to create the kind of culture that helps every player—and every coach—be their very best." I wasn't sure that was the answer DC wanted. Actually, I was sure it *wasn't.*

"Unity isn't only about everyone rallying around the same message; it's also about rallying around one another. This is one team, not offense versus defense, vets versus rookies, or my guys versus your guys." Whit's face reddened.

"You are *one team*," I reiterated. "What *one* of you does affects *all* of you. One unit's success is everyone's success. You win as a team, and you lose as a team. No finger-pointing and no excuses."

You could hear a pin drop. I stole a quick glance at Terry, who nodded in agreement. Whit and DC kept their heads down, eyes glued to their screens. Every other eye in the room was locked in on me.

"You guys are the model. You set the standard. It's your job to make sure that everyone feels like an equal and valuable member of the organization."

"It's hard to feel like an equal and valuable member of the team when you have to get dressed in a separate locker room every week," Stan chimed in.

"At least your guys *have* a locker room," Wilson called. "Look at the practice squad. They might as well be renting out lockers at the Y."

"Okay, settle down, guys," I said. They were just starting to get it, and I didn't want to veer off course.

"Yes," I concurred, "you've got some spatial limitations at the moment." I looked over at Gym, who shrugged helplessly.

"And I'm not sure what would be the best way to address that. Right now, however, your focus needs to be on getting everyone to rally around the same message."

"And what message is that?" asked Joe.

I took a deep breath, then exhaled. "That's what the last letter is for."

• • • • •

"Okay," I said, rubbing my hands together, "I've saved the best for last."

Wilson leaned over and whispered not so quietly to Stan, "How does *L* equal *message*?"

"I'm glad you asked, Coach," I replied. "Actually, it doesn't. The *L* encapsulates everything this team is trying to accomplish. Why it exists. What it stands for."

"Lombardi Trophy?" Gym suggested.

I had to admit—that had never occurred to me. "Nope," I chuckled. "Something even bigger."

"What's bigger than the Lombardi?" came Joe's retort.

"That's just it," I shot back. "It's something beyond trophies and signing bonuses. It's what drives you. It's what gives meaning and significance to what you do every day. The *L* stands for *larger purpose*."

The room was quiet, and a sea of blank expressions stared back at me.

Finally a voice broke in. It was Terry, of all people. "Okay, so what does that mean exactly?"

"Well," I explained, "take charitable organizations or non-profits, for example. People generally work for them because the organizations are built around something they feel is very important. Their goals involve the larger purposes those individuals want to fulfill. They're not just working for a paycheck;

they're contributing to something bigger, more important, and more valuable, and that makes what they do feel more meaningful."

Now Gym spoke up. "That's nice and all, Tony, but what does feeling good about yourself have to do with winning football games?"

"For one thing, when you know that what you're doing is directly impacting others, you tend to try a little harder."

Gym looked dubious. "We're trying to win football games. Not sure I see the connection there."

I was surprised. The last time Lauren and I were with Gym and Ellen, we had discussed this concept. He'd obviously forgotten.

"Coach Noll had a saying: 'Mercenaries will defeat draftees, but the volunteers will crush them both,'" I said. "When I was playing for him, I never quite understood it, but when I joined the coaching staff, I began to understand. His point was that there are three ways to build your army. You can draft people, you can hire people to fight for you, or you can have people enlist. When times get tough, those who are there only because they're forced to be are the first to throw in the towel. Those who see fighting as their way to make a living will hang in a little longer, but when their lives are on the line, they'll have second thoughts because their lives are more important to them than money. But the volunteers, the ones who enlist because they love their country, will fight against all odds because they *believe* in the cause.

"Coach Noll's point was that when we were scouting players, there would be some who were talented and played the game because they were good at it. There would be some who were motivated because of the money they could make from professional football and the lifestyle it could provide. But he wanted us to look for the players who really *loved* the game and were motivated by the enjoyment of being part of the team.

"And once we selected players, Coach Noll's statement took on another meaning. When things got difficult and players were only doing the things we asked them to do because we forced them to do it, it wouldn't seem worth it. Money is a great incentive, but even financial motivation has limits when you're asking people to make tremendous physical and emotional sacrifices. To win a championship, we would need to have people who really bought into what we were doing because they bought into *why* we were doing things—they 'enlisted' because they believed in our larger purpose.

"Enlisted players will recognize that your larger purpose will impact others," I said. "When I was in Pittsburgh, ten thousand people would show up for a Saturday practice during training camp. Joe, you've seen that." Joe nodded. "Some fans would schedule their vacations around training camp because they couldn't afford season tickets, and it was the only chance they'd have to see us play in person. Knowing how much our team meant to the community gave us all an extra incentive to work that much harder. Yeah, we wanted to win—but not just for ourselves. We didn't want to let our *community* down."

"You mean it's harder to be selfish," Wilson piped in.

"You could say that, yes."

"And if you know that others are depending on you, you're more likely to put in the extra effort—to own your effort and attitude," Terry added.

"Exactly."

"And if everyone's committed to the same larger purpose, it brings everyone closer together—makes them more unified," said Joe.

I nodded, then turned back to Gym. "Now do you see why it

matters? It's all interconnected." I walked back over to the whiteboard and pointed at the word *SOUL*. "Teams that exemplify the principles of selflessness, ownership, and unity—teams working toward a larger purpose—are naturally stronger, healthier, more productive, more dedicated, and more successful."

A low rumble filled the room as everyone shared their thoughts and reactions. Terry called out from the back, "So, Tony, what should our larger purpose be?"

I knew that was coming.

"I'm afraid I can't answer that." I shrugged. "I'm just here to visit. You all are the stakeholders in this. You've got skin in the game, so that's something you're going to have to wrestle with together." You could almost feel the air come out of the room.

Straightforward, but not easy.

"But if you can find the right *L*," I said encouragingly, "I think you'll discover that *selflessness*, *ownership*, and *unity* will follow. It might take a little time," I cautioned, "and there will probably be a few bumps in the road. Still, I'm telling you—if this team can find its SOUL . . . the sky's the limit."

PART II

The Plan

It's All Fun and Games

"ALL RIGHT, JUSTIN, remember to square your body and just meet the ball with the bat. Keep your hands soft. Think of the bat absorbing the pitch."

We'd been outside practicing bunting for about twenty minutes, and Justin almost had it down pat. Then just as I was getting ready to toss him another pitch, he dropped his bat to the ground and said, "Dad, I don't want to play anymore."

It had been a tough couple of weeks. His team had lost their last four games, two in extra innings. They were still in the middle of the pack, but barring something unexpected, there was no way they were going to make it to the championship game. It didn't help that Tampa had been having one of the hottest summers in years, so even the night games were brutal.

"All right, buddy," I said, taking off my glove. "We probably should call it a night. It's pretty miserable out here anyway."

"No," he moaned. "I mean I don't want to play *on the team* anymore."

"*What?*" This wasn't like him. "Why not?"

"Because we keep losing." He kicked at the ground. "It's not fun anymore."

Wow. I hadn't seen that coming. I mean, I could understand his frustration. Nobody likes to lose, Justin especially. He was definitely like his older brother Eric. Of course, both of them were like me in that regard. But whether winning or losing, he'd made a commitment to his team. Between his mood and the heat, however, I could tell he wasn't up for a lecture on responsibility. Frankly, neither was I.

I'm going to have to go about this another way.

"Okay." I bent down and started picking up the extra balls around my feet. "I guess you're going to miss seeing your friends, though, huh?"

He cocked his head to the side. "What do you mean?"

"Well, they'll all be at practice most nights and at games every Saturday." His mouth dropped open.

"I'm going to miss it myself," I said, tossing a ball into the equipment bag. "I was really enjoying all those postgame trips to McDonald's and practicing out here with you after school. Of course, we could still hang out doing this, even without a team . . ." I glanced at him out of the corner of my eye. The wheels were starting to turn.

"You were getting pretty good too. Your batting average is up, and you're turning into a really good bunter."

He looked down at the ground. He hated bunting and preferred to swing away. But if he could just put the ball in play, nine times out of ten—with his speed—he could beat out the throw by a good two steps.

"Plus your mom and I both love coming out to watch you play every weekend. So do your brothers and sisters."

He glanced back up at me.

"And I'm sure your coach and your teammates will be

disappointed." I continued tossing balls into the bag. "You're one of their best players." I tilted my head slightly. "I'm sure they'll hate to lose you."

He stared quietly at me for a few seconds, then bent over and picked up his bat. "Okay," he said, resting the bat on his shoulder. "Just three more pitches."

I reached into the bag and grabbed a ball. *That's what I'm talking about.*

WINS AND LOSSES

THE VIPERS HAD BEGUN THE LAST DAY of their organized team activities (OTAs), part of their off-season training regimen, and I'd just arrived at the stadium to take care of a few loose ends before Lauren, the kids, and I headed out west for a month.

Justin's Little League team had finished strong, winning their last three games. He played a key role in one of them, laying down a perfect sacrifice bunt in the seventh inning and advancing the winning run. It had been a long, sometimes frustrating season, but Justin had grown tremendously, as both a player and a teammate.

Now we were looking forward to a relaxing family vacation together. Lauren and I had put the kids in charge of the itinerary, so for the past several weeks, they'd been knee-deep in materials on Bryce Canyon, Arches, and other Utah national parks. I had brought a couple of mock itineraries the kids had put together the night before in case I had time to look at them. As soon as I turned the corner toward my office, however, I saw Terry, Gym, and Joe pacing nervously outside the door. I knew the national parks were going to have to wait.

"Well, you guys are certainly looking for supplies early this morning," I said with a smile. No one laughed. They all looked edgy—especially Terry.

Gym took a step forward. "We've got a problem, Tony."

"Okay." I glanced at my office door and chuckled. "I'd invite you in, but I'm not sure we'd all fit."

"Why don't we meet in my office?" Joe offered. I half expected someone to fill me in as we walked, but all eyes seemed to be fixed on the floor. As soon as we settled in Joe's office, however, the floodgates opened.

"This isn't working," Joe began.

"What isn't working?" I asked. I hadn't been out to the stadium much in the last couple of weeks, but from what I could tell, things seemed to be running smoothly. Joe and his staff had outlined the SOUL philosophy with the team, and for the most part, everyone seemed very receptive. They had even decorated the locker room with banners and signs that read "Vipers Have SOUL," and some enterprising player had written "Food" on a sheet of paper and taped it to the end of one of the banners. Of course, I'd been around long enough to know that major philosophic change doesn't just happen overnight.

"SOUL isn't working," Joe continued, the frustration evident in his voice. "Today is the last day of OTAs, but we're not getting any better at the whole teamwork thing." Gym and Terry both looked concerned.

I listened as Joe continued his rant. "We've told them to 'play with SOUL'—in meetings and at practice—until we're blue in the face. It works for a play or two, but then the guys who've been dogging it go right back to the same old lazy plays— sloppy footwork by linemen, receivers rounding their routes instead of making sharp cuts at precise spots, guys jogging to where they need to be—"

"They're just not getting it," Gym broke in. "They all know what they're supposed to do. They all agree with what we laid out, but then . . ."

"It's just not happening," Terry finished.

I'd figured this moment would come. The hard truth is that it's a lot easier to paint a slogan on the wall or parrot a new catchphrase than to be consistently intentional about the direction an organization is heading—and then to actually *move* in that direction. The good news was that they seemed to have absorbed the principles of SOUL I had outlined the previous month, and I'd been encouraged in the weeks that followed by all the chatter I was hearing around the building about selflessness and unity and the importance of everyone owning their role on the field. What I hadn't heard, though—what they *weren't* talking about—was *why* they were doing it and what it all meant.

They weren't talking about the *L*.

•　　•　　•　　•　　•

"Let me ask—" I glanced around the room at the three frustrated faces staring back at me—"the last time we talked about this, you still hadn't landed on a larger purpose for this team— something everyone could rally around. Have you come up with anything yet?" The sheepish expressions on their faces gave me my answer.

"Well," Joe began, "we certainly want to make the playoffs."

"And do better than we did last year," Gym continued.

"And we want to sustain that year after year," Terry added.

"So, in a word, *win*," I said. They looked at each other and nodded.

"Why?" I asked.

All three opened their mouths as if to speak but then fell

silent. Confused glances were exchanged; then Terry broke in. "What do you mean?"

"*Why* do you want to win?" I asked.

More confused glances.

"Look, *everyone* wants to win. But is that the only reason you guys got involved in football?"

Nothing.

I turned to Terry. "Terry, you had a long and successful career as a judge before you came here." He nodded. "So why did you leave?"

"I don't know." He paused for a second, seemingly thrown by the question. "I guess it's because I've always loved the game and wanted a new challenge. You know I played all through high school and college. Law school was plan B when I finally realized I didn't have a future in the NFL," he said with a wink.

"And I like working with people," he said, glancing in Gym and Joe's direction, "and solving problems." He looked up and met my gaze. "Plus, I've always loved Orlando. Owen is a good friend of mine, and I really liked the idea of helping him get this team off the ground."

"So . . . you didn't come here *to win*?" I prodded him.

"Well, I don't want to *lose*," he shot back.

"No, of course not," I replied. "But it wasn't *just* the idea of winning that brought you here."

"Well . . ." He hesitated for a moment. "No," he admitted.

"How about you, Gym?" I asked. "You left a strong organization in Detroit—three straight playoff seasons, if I'm remembering correctly. Why are you here?"

Gym, who for as long as I'd known him had never enjoyed being the center of attention, shifted uncomfortably in his chair. "Same as Terry, I guess. Detroit was a great organization, but there was something about the idea of helping a new team get off the ground—being there at the beginning—building something." A smile crept across his face. "Plus, Ellen and I are both from Orlando originally. It's a great community, and it would be nice to give something back."

"It wasn't just about winning for you either, then."

He shook his head.

"Well, I *do* want to win," Joe broke in.

"Of course you do," I agreed. "So do Terry and Gym. Everyone—no matter what business or industry they're in—wants to succeed. What I'm trying to zero in on here is what's driving your will to succeed. *Why* do you want to win?"

Joe looked completely flummoxed—and a little annoyed.

"Because I'm a football coach," he shot back. "It's my *job* to win."

"Right. And it's Terry's job to bring in the best coaching and support staff he can find." I nodded at Terry, then at Gym. "And it's Gym's job to manage the day-to-day operations and take care of player personnel. That's *what* they do. But you heard them just now. What motivates them—what gives their work meaning—is bigger than their limited job descriptions, or even their day-to-day jobs. It's about helping to create something—in a sport they both love, in a city they both love. That's *why* they're here. That's *why* they do what they do. Does that make sense?"

Terry and Gym both nodded in agreement. Joe, however, still looked skeptical.

"But I *do* want to win," he protested. "That *is* what motivates me."

It was obvious I needed to take a different tack here. I sat back in my chair while Joe continued to stare me down. It was like déjà vu all over again.

That's when it hit me. I leaned forward and gestured to the

pictures on the wall behind Joe's desk—the ones of him with Don Shula and Bill Walsh.

"Joe, when we first talked this spring, you said you had hoped to join Don and Bill in the Hall of Fame someday, right?"

"Of course," he scoffed. "Who wouldn't?"

"What is it about those two that you admire?"

He swiveled his chair around to look at the pictures. "They were fantastic coaches. I mean, Bill engineered the West Coast offense in San Francisco and completely turned that franchise around. Shula was—*is*—the winningest coach in NFL history. And he went to six Super Bowls," he added triumphantly. "Six!"

"Didn't he lose four of those Super Bowls?" Terry asked—not as a criticism—just checking his facts, as any former judge is wont to do. I was glad he did.

Joe's head snapped around so quickly you could almost hear the tendons snap. "That's not the point!" he barked. "The guy was an offensive and defensive genius! He's the one who brought the 3-4 defense to the league!"

"He also makes one amazing steak," Gym joked, bringing a much-needed break in the tension.

"Okay, hold on a second," I jumped in. "Joe, you just said that Don losing more Super Bowls than he's won wasn't the point. Why is that?"

He shifted in his chair as he thought for a second. "The guy was just a brilliant coach—and one of the best communicators this league has ever had," he calmly stated. "His teams were right there in the mix, year after year after year." He glanced back up at the photo, and in a much more reflective tone, added, "Guys just loved playing for him."

"He definitely left quite a legacy," I said. "Both of them did. In fact, it sounds to me like *that's* what you admire most about them. Not just the wins, but also the impact they had on the league, the innovations they brought to the game, and the way they inspired everyone around them. *That's* why it doesn't matter to you that he lost more Super Bowls than he won."

Joe nodded, silently staring at the photos.

"Come to think of it," Gym piped back in, "as long as we're talking about the Dolphins . . . Dan Marino is probably one of the best quarterbacks ever to play the game, and he never got a ring."

"No, he never did." I hadn't been thinking about Marino. "There are a lot of great players and head coaches who never won the Super Bowl: Marv Levy, Bud Grant, Jim Kelly, Barry Sanders . . ." I listed them off. "That doesn't mean they weren't great at what they did, or that they didn't make an impact." I glanced over at Joe just in time to catch a subtle nod of recognition.

"I guess what I'm trying to say, Joe, is that winning *is* important. But by your own admission, what you admire most about Don Shula and Bill Walsh—what you're trying to emulate—is not so much their records but the way they changed the game and the impact they had on those around them. You want to win, yes. But you also want to be a great coach—the kind of guy people will respect, play hard for, and model themselves after. You want to leave a legacy of excellence behind. *That's* what drives you."

"Yeah . . . Plus, it would be great to see Orlando establish itself as an NFL powerhouse. Nothing against Miami, Tampa, or Jacksonville, but Orlando is a great sports town too. I'd love to see this city win a championship."

Now they're getting it.

"So . . . Joe's *L* is building a legacy of excellence and success, and Gym's is helping to build a successful franchise from the ground up," Terry concluded. He glanced at Gym, who gave a thumbs-up.

"And it sounds like that's yours, too," Gym said to Terry.

"Yeah." Terry smiled. "I guess it is." He looked more animated than I'd seen him in weeks. "Okay, so we all hope to build something successful that will have a positive impact on others . . ."

"And we all want to give something back to the community," Gym added.

"Definitely. So is that it?" Terry looked at me expectantly.

"It's definitely a start," I said. "But . . ."

"What about everyone else?" Gym realized, finishing my thought. "You said that part of what gives a team a SOUL is that everyone shares a larger purpose—something they can *all* rally around."

"That's why just telling the guys to 'play with SOUL' isn't working," Joe said as he took off his hat and ran a hand through his hair.

Terry elaborated. "There's nothing holding this team together. Nothing driving them."

All three men bowed their heads while I just sat quietly and let them think. They had done a remarkable job of connecting the dots up to this point. And the truth is, they were a lot closer than they realized. Suddenly Joe's head shot up, a spark of realization in his eyes.

"This isn't just about us," he said, looking squarely at Terry and Gym. "We need to talk to the team."

"And Owen," said Gym.

"Yes," Terry concurred. "Definitely Owen."

I leaned back in my chair and smiled.

Now that's what I'm talking about.

Don't Kill
the Messenger

While Gym, Joe, and Terry scrambled to find as many players as they could to speak into the team's goals, I went back to my office to take care of a few odds and ends. I had to admit, I hadn't been expecting quite this much excitement on the last day of OTAs, but it was encouraging to see the three of them working so diligently and so closely together to implement the changes we had talked about.

I had just settled in behind my desk and picked up the kids' vacation itineraries when Mark King, the head of the marketing department, knocked on my door.

"Hey, Tony," he said, poking his head around the door, "got a second?"

Mark had interned at NFL headquarters and then with NBC's *Football Night in America*, which is where I'd met him. An Orlando native and a graduate of the city's University of Central Florida, he'd been directing the Vipers' marketing efforts for the past three years.

"Of course, Mark, come on in." I set the itineraries back

down on my desk. Once again, the national parks were going to have to wait.

"Thanks." He took a seat, then glanced around the room. "Nice place you've got here," he said with a laugh.

"Thanks, Mark. I like it."

"I've been meaning to stop by and say hello since you started a few months ago, but things have been a little . . ." He paused briefly, searching for the right word.

"Hectic?" I offered.

He slowly nodded. "Yeah . . . ," he said, "let's go with hectic." He glanced down at the papers in front of me. "I'm not interrupting anything, am I?"

"No. Lauren and I are getting ready to take the kids out west for a month, and we put them in charge of the travel plans. We're trying to see how many of the national parks we can visit before school and the season both kick back into gear."

He smiled, zeroing in on one of the drawings Jaela had made. "That sounds great. I can't wait to do that myself someday."

"How's Ashley coming along?" Mark and his wife were expecting their first child later in the summer.

"She's doing great." He was beaming. "Shouldn't be too long now." He ran his hand over his jet-black hair. "We're a little nervous, but both of our families live in the area, so we'll definitely have plenty of help."

"That *does* make a difference."

Mark looked down at his lap. I could tell something was bothering him.

"So how's everything going workwise?" I asked. His eyes met mine, though his chin stayed down. *Uh-oh*, I thought. *That doesn't look promising.*

He took a deep breath and sat back in his seat. "Well, I'm sure by now you've heard how Owen's slipup made it into the papers."

"Oakland?"

He pursed his lips and nodded.

"Yes, I've heard. I'm guessing that didn't help lighten your summer load, did it?"

"Not much, no," he said. "I love my job, Tony, I really do. But trying to sell sponsorships and get fans excited about the team when the owner has all but threatened to pack up and move across the country . . ." His voice trailed off.

"Isn't exactly easy," I finished for him.

"No, it's not," he replied.

"I know it's frustrating, Mark, but try not to let it get you down." I was trying to conjure up a quick pep talk in my head when another thought occurred to me.

"Let me ask you something. If the team *were* to move to Oakland, would you go with them?"

The look he gave me spoke volumes.

"I don't know, Tony. The timing is terrible. Ashley and I were really hoping to put down roots here in Orlando—what with the baby coming and all."

I could certainly understand that. One of the most difficult parts of working in professional sports is the transient nature of the business. Guys get traded midseason and live apart from their families for months on end. Coaching staffs turn over, and the next thing you know, you're packing up your house, and your kids have to say good-bye to all of their friends and start over somewhere else. I'd watched countless coaches and players go through it over the course of my career, and it was never easy. Moving an entire franchise, though, would affect everyone in the organization—marketing, public relations, accounting, and other support staff. It takes an awful lot of people to make a team this size run effectively day in and day out.

"I just wish there was a way to convince Mr. Joyce to stay in Orlando," he added wistfully. "This is a great city, and this could be a terrific franchise. We've got good weather, accessible transportation, world-class amenities . . . We could easily host a Super Bowl here . . ." Then he caught himself. "*If* we had a decent stadium."

I jumped in to build on his comments. "Now wait a minute, Mark. Nothing's been decided yet. Plus, there are real benefits to staying—you and your team have done a phenomenal job establishing the Vipers brand here." And they had. The Vipers boasted one of the most recognizable logos in the NFL, and their merchandise sales had consistently ranked in the top five in each of the three years the team had existed, right alongside the Cowboys, Steelers, Packers, and Raiders.

"My son Justin *lives* in his Vipers gear," I laughed, gesturing toward a recent family photo with Justin standing front and center wearing his Austin jersey. "You're one of the best marketing guys in this league."

"Thanks, Tony. I appreciate it. Like I said, I love my job. I just wish there was something more I could do to help."

Before I could say anything, Gym poked his head around the door. "Hey, Tony, sorry to interrupt," he said, glancing at Mark, "but Joe was able to grab a handful of guys from the locker room before they left. You available?"

I looked at Mark. "I'm sorry, Mark. I need to step out for a few minutes. Could we pick this up again later today—maybe after lunch?"

"Absolutely," he said, pushing back his chair to clear a path for me.

"Actually, Tony," Gym interjected, "Terry was able to get Owen to clear about an hour for us today after lunch, and I was kind of hoping you could be there."

I turned toward Mark, who smiled back at me. "Sounds like you've got your hands full today," he said.

"I'm afraid I do," I replied, rising to my feet. Then something occurred to me. "Mark, what are you doing this afternoon?"

He shrugged. "Nothing that can't be changed. Why?"

I turned to Gym. "Would it be okay with you if Mark joined us this afternoon? I think it might be helpful."

Gym and Mark exchanged glances. Then Gym shrugged. "It's fine by me."

"Excellent." I clapped a hand down on Mark's shoulder. "There just might be something you can do to help after all."

A FEW GOOD MEN

By THE TIME GYM AND I ARRIVED in the personnel meeting room, Terry and Joe were already there, along with Austin Quarles, Wesley Robinson, and Louis Blackstock.

Interesting group, I thought. Actually, it made a lot of sense. As the starting quarterback and team captain, Austin was a natural leader who automatically commanded a great deal of respect. And Louis was a linebacker, widely regarded as one of the best defensive players in the NFC and the closest thing the Vipers had to a defensive star. The guy was a monster on the field, and DC absolutely loved him. "He plays hurt, never quits, totally fires up the defense, and does everything we ask of him," he had told me during minicamp.

As soon as I walked in the door, both Austin and Louis came over and shook my hand. "Coach," they both said by way of greeting.

As for the rookie . . .

"Nice to meet you, sir," Wesley said, waiting for Austin and Louis to step back before approaching me and extending his hand.

Louis raised his eyebrows. "Hey, the kid *can* speak!"

Everyone laughed. In the short time he'd been with the team, Wesley had been almost as quiet as Louis was loud. Compared to the fiery and loquacious Louis, Wesley may as well have taken a vow of silence around the facility. He kept his head down and did his job.

"Nice to meet you, too, son. And please, call me Coach," I said, smiling. "*Sir* makes me nervous."

"Yes, sir," he laughed, then apologized. "I'm not sure why *I'm* here," he added, glancing back at Austin and Louis, "but I'm happy to help however I can."

"That's *exactly* why you're here," Joe said, inviting the three players to take a seat at the table. I followed suit.

"You pay attention and you do what we ask, both in the weight room and on the practice field. That's exactly what we need to make this work—leaders," he said emphatically, adding, "and not all leaders have to speak."

"Make what work, Coach?" Austin asked.

"You guys know how we've been talking about becoming a team with SOUL this season, right?" All three nodded in response.

"Well, there's one piece we haven't quite landed on yet, and I think—*we* think—" Joe gestured toward Gym, Terry, and me—"that you guys might be able to help us with that."

"Is it the selflessness thing?" Louis asked. "'Cause I think most of the guys get that. They just might not always do it," he said with a smile.

"And *that's* the problem," Joe said, turning to the whiteboard behind him and grabbing a dry-erase marker.

He continued to speak while starting to write on the board. "I agree, Louis—we can already do selflessness. Most of us, most of the time. Some of us, not so often. And we're pretty good at owning our roles," he added. "Again, most of the time."

"Well, I think we're pretty unified," Austin spoke up. "I mean, we all get along well."

"True, when times are good. But—" Joe paused with just *SOU* written on the board—"what is it that unifies us? What drives us to succeed, especially when things get tough?"

Joe turned back around and sketched out the final letter. "What is our *L*? And before you all say, 'Super Bowl,'" he continued, "that's not it."

The guys exchanged confused glances. Joe turned to me. "Tony, would you mind?"

"Not at all." I got up and walked over to the whiteboard. "First of all, Coach Webster is spot-on. The Super Bowl is a great goal, and I have no doubt you guys can get there, but in all my years in the league, I've found the most consistently successful teams are driven by something even bigger than that."

"What's bigger than the Super Bowl?" asked Wesley.

"Whoa, he spoke twice in one day!" Louis teased, bringing a flush of red to the rookie's cheeks.

"The Super Bowl is *what* we want to achieve," Joe interjected.

I picked up from there. "Right. But what we're talking about is what gives meaning to what you do here; what defines *who you are* as individuals and as a team—regardless of whether you win the Super Bowl. Winning is important, yes. But *how* and *why* you win are equally—if not *more*—important. Because without *meaning*, gentlemen, I can promise you—even your greatest victories will ring hollow."

Terry and Gym nodded in agreement.

"Austin," Joe said, turning to his team captain, "why do you want to win the Super Bowl?"

The quarterback thought for a few seconds, then said, "I guess I want to win for the fans. We didn't have a lot of money when I was growing up, and my brothers and I all loved football.

My dad worked overtime every week for a year just to take us to one game a season. I'm sure a lot of our fans are in the same boat. You kind of want to reward that, ya know? Show them how much you appreciate their support, not just by winning, but also by playing your hardest every day."

"What about you, Louis?" I asked.

"I guess I want to win it for the rest of the guys on the team. Everyone works so hard all year. Guys are constantly playing hurt. We're on the road a lot, away from our families. Everyone sacrifices so much . . ." He paused, then added thoughtfully, "I'd like to honor that."

"Man, I've never even *been* to an NFL game," Wesley chimed in, drawing surprised looks from both of his teammates. "We couldn't afford it either." Then he looked at me. "I'd like to win for my old coaches back in Tennessee. Make 'em proud. Show all the other guys playing in Division II and III programs that they can make it too, if they work hard."

I looked over at Joe. "You've got a great group here, Coach." I could tell from Joe's expression that he had been genuinely moved by the humility his little handpicked trio had just demonstrated, but the hard-as-nails coach quickly shook it off.

"Okay," he said, scribbling on the board, "so we've got 'Win for each other,' 'Win for the fans,' and 'Win to inspire others.'"

Relationships, community building, and legacy. I smiled to myself and wondered whether Gym, Terry, and Joe realized that the players had landed on the same themes they had identified earlier this morning.

After studying the list for a few seconds, Joe turned back to his players. "What do you guys think?"

Once again, Austin spoke first. "Well, I think I can speak for most of the guys on the offense, and I can't think of anyone who would disagree with that."

"Yeah," Louis affirmed. "I think the defense would get behind that, too."

All eyes turned to the rookie.

"What do you think, Wesley?" Terry asked. Wesley scanned the board, took a deep breath, smiled, and nodded.

"Now *that's* the Wesley I'm used to," Louis laughed, shoving the rookie so hard he almost fell out of his chair.

"So, Coach, what can we do to help?" Austin asked.

Joe turned back to me, so I stepped forward. "Austin and Louis, you guys are two of the leaders of this team. There are others, of course, but we wanted to bounce it off you first."

Louis grinned. "Plus, we were still there when you came to the locker room."

"Yes, but that underscores the point," Joe said. "Quite often you're the first to arrive and the last to leave. The other guys look up to you. They listen to you. They watch the way you act, the way you carry yourselves—on the field, in the weight room, in front of the media, in the community, with the fans, and with each other."

He looked at me, and I picked up the thread. "Your job is to model these principles," I said, pointing back at the board. "Keep them front and center at all times. Help get—and *keep*—everybody on board. Remind them why they're here, what they represent, what they're playing for—*who* they're playing for.

"And you, Wesley, are here because you already model these things: not putting yourself first, doing with passion whatever you're asked, pulling for others. Anyone can influence others—which is all leadership is." I didn't add, *Even a late-round draft pick not guaranteed to make the team.* They all knew it, though. Even Wesley.

"What if certain guys don't buy into it?" Austin asked.

I'd been waiting for someone to ask that. "Great question."

"We'll make 'em," Louis cut in. Everybody laughed.

"Well, that might work for a little while, Louis. But you guys are right. Unfortunately, not everyone always buys in. What we're trying to do here is create an environment that models, encourages, and celebrates selfless play and fully owning your role—not just the things you *like* to do, but all of it. We want to see everyone working together as one unified team—not us versus them, offense versus defense, or one guy against the world. It's about being driven by our desire to serve one another, our fans, and everyone who looks up to us. If we can create that kind of environment, most people will climb on board.

"But if a guy's out of line to the point where it's becoming detrimental to the team or having a negative impact on the overall culture you're trying to create—" I paused, took a deep breath, and looked over at Joe, Gym, and Terry—"that's when you have to think about making a change."

"That's pretty harsh," Louis said, nodding solemnly.

"It *can* be," I agreed.

"I guess if it were easy, everyone would be doing it," Austin concluded.

"Exactly," I said.

The room was quiet for a few seconds as everyone mulled over what had just transpired. Then Joe broke the silence.

"So," he began, a note of challenge in his voice, "you guys up to it?"

Austin and Louis both nodded their heads enthusiastically, but Wesley looked a little unsure of himself. I couldn't say that I blamed him. It had to feel awkward.

"What do you think, Wesley?" I said in the same tone I often used to nudge my own kids into making a tough decision. "Remember, you don't have to say a word. Some of the most effective leadership simply comes from our behavior."

He looked from face to face for a second, expressionless, before a slow smile began to spread across his face.

"You know what the Good Book says, Coach." He began paraphrasing Luke 12:48, one of my favorite Bible verses. "To whom much has been given . . ."

The kid knows his Scripture.

I smiled as I finished the verse. "Much will be required."

How about that, I thought. *I think the Vipers may have just found their SOUL.*

THE MAN UPSTAIRS

THE LUNCH BREAK FINALLY GAVE ME a chance to sit down and look through the itineraries the kids had created. I was genuinely impressed with how much time and effort they had put into them, and I told Lauren as much when I called her.

"You know, they really did a great job researching all of this stuff. Which one of them figured out the mileage?"

"I'm not sure," she said, "but whoever it was is definitely *your* child."

I just laughed.

"So how's the last day going?" Lauren asked.

"Busier than I expected, but encouraging," I told her. "I think they're really starting to buy in to the concept. In fact, we're on our way to meet with Owen in a few minutes to get his input on what we—" I quickly corrected myself—"on what *they've* come up with."

"That's great, hon. What time do you expect to be home?"

Just as I was about to answer, Mark appeared at my door. When he saw that I was on the phone, he quietly waved and took a step back.

"I should be home by four at the latest. Do you need me to grab anything on my way?"

"Nope. We're good. Say hi to Owen for me."

"Will do," I said. "See you in a bit."

"Sorry, about that, Tony," Mark apologized, edging his way back into the room.

"Oh, don't worry about it," I assured him. "I was just touching base with Lauren about the trip."

"Yeah?" his eyes lit up. "What did you decide?"

"I think we're going to go with plan C," I said, holding up one of the information packets. "We won't cover as much ground, but we'll have more time to spend at each spot."

"Quality over quantity." Mark smiled.

"Exactly," I agreed. "You all set?" I stood up, grabbed a legal pad off one of the shelves, and headed toward the door.

"Yep." He looked a little nervous.

To be honest, I was a little anxious myself. The last time I'd spoken with Owen, he was dead set on either filling his trophy case or leaving town. Since his slipup with the press, he hadn't exactly been the most popular figure in the building, either. Still, I knew that Terry had brought him up to speed on what we'd been talking about, so I figured there was at least a chance he had softened a little.

"Come on," I said, smiling and clapping Mark on the back. "Terry and the others are going to meet us upstairs."

Mark took a deep breath. "What's the worst that can happen, right?" he said with a shaky smile.

Good question.

• • • • •

When Mark and I arrived at Owen's office, Terry, Gym, and Joe were all seated on a leather sectional in front of the windows overlooking the field. Owen was nowhere in sight.

Gym waved us in. "Come on in. Owen just stepped out to take a call."

Mark and I each took a seat in one of the matching leather chairs that had been moved over by the sectional. This time, however, I made a point of sitting on the edge of the seat. Mark, unfortunately, quickly found himself sinking into the leather abyss that had caught me by surprise my first time here.

"Planning to stay awhile?" Gym asked as Mark struggled to pull himself back into an upright position.

"Yes, actually, I am." Mark winked back at him, righting himself.

"Mark's hoping he can help us convince Owen to stay in Orlando," I explained.

"Really?" Terry sounded hopeful. "What's your plan?"

Mark inched forward in his seat and opened his mouth as if to speak, but before he could get a word out, Owen burst into the room, a smile a mile wide lighting up his face.

"Great news, gentlemen," he announced as he clapped his hands in front of him. "I just got off the phone with our attorney, and it looks as though the city has approved the proposed deal points for our new stadium."

Terry shot me a surprised look. In the aftermath of the Oakland firestorm, he mentioned that he and Owen had quietly presented members of the city council with a prospective proposal for the upcoming referendum ballot—but I got the impression he didn't think it would happen at all, and certainly not this quickly.

"Are you serious?" Terry asked.

"Yes, sir," Owen replied. "They're going to put the new tax on February's special-election ballot." He turned toward the field. "Now we just need to win enough games to keep people excited so they will vote in favor of the tax."

Mark, Gym, Joe, and I all exchanged glances. Owen's announcement seemed like an answer to prayer. Terry jumped back in.

"So they didn't change *any* of the deal points?" Terry asked.

"Nope, not one," Owen declared triumphantly. "Of course, they weren't exactly thrilled with all of them. But they know they stand to lose *a lot* more if this team moves to Oakland."

Hmm . . . I didn't like the sound of that. And from the looks of it, neither did Terry.

"What, exactly, are the deal points?" I asked, looking back and forth between the two of them.

Terry sighed. "The team will contribute one-eighth of the new stadium's construction costs . . ."

"Which, of course, we can borrow from the league," Owen interjected.

"Who pays for the rest?" asked Mark.

"Basically, the city has to pay for whatever the state won't," Terry explained.

"Which could be the entire amount," I said, the full realization of Terry's hesitant response sinking in. Under this structure, Owen would make out like a bandit, but the city—and ultimately, the fans—would probably lose big-time, like most stadium deals.

"Right," Terry responded.

"Why is that?" asked Joe.

"The governor wasn't exactly thrilled when we threatened to pull the team from Orlando," Terry explained.

Mark, who had spent his entire summer swimming upstream against the backlash of Owen's threat, nodded, no doubt at the recollection of the governor's now infamous "Don't let the door hit you on your way out" comment.

"But that's not a problem for us," Owen broke in, "because the city will just pick up the rest of the tab. So either way, we win."

Terry's eyes met mine. I could read his thoughts like a book. *Do we?*

"What about the city?" Mark asked. "Would they be able to use the stadium?"

"Of course!" Owen exclaimed. "They'd be welcome to use the stadium for college or high school games, concerts, expos, you name it."

Well, that's something at least.

"But," Owen continued, "we'd have full veto power."

Or maybe not.

"For instance," he explained, "let's say Orlando wants to keep hosting the Citrus State Showdown game every fall. They'd have to come to us for approval first."

"Which we would grant, of course," Terry interjected hopefully. The Showdown was an annual matchup between two small, historically African American universities located in Florida. The event gave both programs a helpful jolt of exposure, and all proceeds went to support their scholarship funds.

"Of course," Owen boomed. "Unless we had a game the next day. I mean we wouldn't want the grass to get torn up the day before a game."

Everyone went silent. On the one hand, Owen had a point. Nobody likes to play on ripped-up turf. But breaking a community tradition that had stood for more than a decade certainly wouldn't paint the Vipers in a very favorable light.

"But at least the schools or the city would get part of the proceeds from concession sales," Mark said.

"Actually," Owen continued, "under the proposed plan, we would get all concession profits from *any* events held in the stadium—high school games, concerts, the Citrus State Showdown, whatever. Any money for parking too."

A whistle escaped my lips. "That's a lot."

"You bet it is," Owen smiled. "Plus, we'd get revenues from the stadium's naming rights and all in-stadium advertising."

Wow, I thought, *that's a truly terrible deal for Orlando.*

I tried to take a quick read of the room. Owen, clearly, was ecstatic. But of course he would be. He was in a position to get the new stadium he wanted without it costing him a cent. He stood to make a tidy profit to boot, and he would be a hero for staying in Orlando.

Mark was a little harder to read. On the one hand, if the city voted yes, he and his family would be able to stay in Orlando. But I could almost see the wheels turning as he thought about trying to sell sponsorships to local businesses who would have to know what a lousy deal it was. And there was a chance fans wouldn't see the team in a positive light over the deal, either. It might not be a big marketing win.

Terry was clearly disappointed the city had conceded to such a one-sided deal. I could tell from his expression that his sense of justice and fairness had taken a swift hit, but he was doing his best to think about it from his employer's standpoint, as was Gym.

Joe looked as if he'd had the wind knocked out him—all the excitement and enthusiasm from our earlier meetings was completely drained from his face. I was seeing a sensitive side of the head coach that he didn't often let slip. I had a feeling Austin's and Wesley's comments were weighing on him, reminding him how difficult it already was for most families to afford tickets.

A quick glance at Owen told me he had also been taking stock of the room, and he wasn't happy with the lukewarm reception his news had garnered.

"Why the long faces?" he challenged. "I thought you all wanted to stay in Orlando. If this plan passes, we'll be able to do that."

Everyone remained silent, and several concerned glances were exchanged before Gym finally spoke up.

"But at what cost, Owen? I mean, yes, the team would get to stay in Orlando, but even you have to admit that this is a pretty one-sided deal. It's not very fan friendly, and it won't exactly endear us to the community."

"No, it won't," Mark said. He slowly shook his head, his eyes glued to the floor.

Owen—quite possibly for the first time in his life—was speechless.

Joe quickly jumped in. "Listen, Owen, we've been talking all morning—we even met with a few of the players—and we think we've finally got the pieces in place to turn the corner and make a drive deep into the playoffs. We might even go all the way, but—"

Before Joe could finish, Owen found his voice. "But nothing, Joe! What is this, a football team or a popularity contest?" he said with a snort. "I come in here and tell you guys I may have just gotten us the deal of the century, and you all are worried about the optics of it?"

As the only person in the room who didn't have a career riding on whatever happened next, I decided to step in.

"Owen, I think what Joe and the others are trying to say is that while staying in Orlando is important, one of the values we've been talking a lot about these past few months is the importance of giving something back to the community—honoring the fans by giving them the best we've got each and every day, winning not just for us but also for them, and investing in them the way they've invested in us."

"Sticking the fans with the cost of the stadium while refusing to share any of the profits isn't exactly the best way to start," added a clearly disenchanted Mark.

Sensing that Mark may have just signed his own dismissal papers, Terry quickly jumped in. "Owen, Mark may have spoken out of turn, but he does raise an excellent point. Just because the city approved the proposal doesn't guarantee that the voters will. And Gym's right, it *is* going to be a tough sell. Maybe if we revisited—"

"Look, gentlemen—" Owen was clearly exasperated—"we don't need to revisit anything. Our fans love us. Just look at our merchandise sales! They're through the roof! You just win us some games, boys," he said, pointing at Joe and Gym. Glancing at Mark, he added, "And you line up some big-time sponsors for us."

Turning to me, he said, "Tony, whatever you need to do to inspire this team, you go ahead and do it, because this ballot measure has got to pass." He pointed toward the field. "We need the taxpayers to cover that last seven-eighths, or—mark my words, gentlemen—this franchise will move."

The room fell silent. Then Terry calmly rose to his feet and said, "We hear you, Owen. We'll do our best."

Owen, to his credit, responded with a genuine smile and a much calmer tone.

"That's all I'm asking, Terry."

We politely thanked Owen for his time and filed out into the hall. As soon as we were out of earshot, Gym turned to me and sighed. "He doesn't get it, does he?"

"Not yet. But then, neither did any of you right away," I

reminded them. "Owen's a good guy. And he really does love this city. Just give him a little time. He'll get there."

"What happens if he doesn't?" asked Mark.

"I guess we'll cross that bridge when we come to it," grumbled Joe.

Gym scoffed. "Yeah, let's just hope it's not the San Francisco–Oakland Bay Bridge."

"Hang in there, guys," I said. "Hang in there."

PART III

The Progress

TRAINING CAMP

"ARE YOU SURE WE CAN'T STAY A LITTLE LONGER?" Justin had managed to talk his way into accompanying me to the first full day of training camp, and he had spent the better part of the hour-long drive lobbying to stay with the team at Orlando's Rollins College for the entire week.

While I was flattered that Justin still wanted to tag along after spending the better part of three weeks cooped up with me in an RV driving through the American West, there was no way I was signing either of us on for a full week of training camp. I'd been to thirty-three monthlong training camps over the course of my career. Added together, that was almost three years of my life spent sleeping in a dorm away from my family, and that was plenty in my book—even if we were talking about a dorm room on the upscale Rollins campus.

"We agreed to one night," I reminded him. "Besides, those guys have *a lot* of work to do." And they did. Coming in to training camp, the roster was sitting at ninety players, well above the fifty-three the team would take into the regular season. I didn't envy all the long hours and late nights awaiting the coaching staff—or the sleepless nights for players still competing for a chance to wear the green and black. Only a handful of guys were guaranteed places on the roster; the rest were still in danger: draft picks, high-priced free agents, and last season's starters included.

Even Wesley, already one of my favorites.

Still, the camp would be a great litmus test to see who was and wasn't buying into the SOUL principles. After all, if there was ever a time for everyone to be giving 100 percent, this was it.

•　•　•　•　•

As soon as we arrived at the athletic facility, we headed over to the main auditorium, where Coach Webster was scheduled to address the team.

The room was packed. Joe, Whit, DC, Stan, and the rest of the coaching staff were all seated up on stage, wearing their green Vipers polos and khaki slacks. I made eye contact with each, nodding as I went, and then steered Justin toward the back of the auditorium. His eyes were like saucers as his head swiveled around trying to catch a glimpse of his favorite player, Austin Quarles. We were just about to take our seats when I spotted Austin sitting front and center in the first row, flanked by Louis Blackstock on one side and Wesley Robinson on the other. *How about that?* I thought. *The trio stuck together.* That was certainly a good sign.

The room fell silent as Joe stood up to speak.

"Good morning, and welcome to Vipers training camp." Even without the benefit of a mic, Joe's voice filled the room.

His opening comments were similar to many of mine over the years: "Last season has no bearing, good or bad, on this season. Just like us, every team is starting over at zero," and so on.

As Joe continued, I noticed that Austin and Louis—both of whom had been through numerous training camps and had no doubt heard similar if not identical talks at each—were both attentively taking notes. It was great to see them setting such a great example for the younger players. In fact, it reminded me of the 49ers training camp I'd sat in on years earlier when future Hall of Famer Joe Montana had done the exact same thing, something he would continue to do every training camp of his career. It wasn't because he needed to remember what Coach Walsh was saying. He'd heard it many times before and had it committed to memory, but by paying attention and taking notes, he was setting a good example for the other players. They needed to see that what Coach was saying was important.

After a few minutes, Joe got around to the concept of teamwork.

"Toward the end of OTAs you heard us talk about becoming a team with SOUL," he said, writing *SOUL* out in big block letters on the rollaway whiteboard behind him. He then laid out a detailed explanation of the four points, much as I'd done in the staff meeting.

"Now, right before we broke for summer, Mr. McKenzie, Mr. Hodges, Coach Dungy, and I sat down with a few of you to talk about our larger purpose. Austin, Louis, Wesley," he gestured toward the front row, "would you guys mind sharing what we came up with?"

Huh, good move having the players talk to the players. I liked that.

As Austin rose to address the team, I noticed that Justin sat up a little taller in his seat.

"Like Coach Webster was saying, it's not enough just to say we want to win, because at the end of the day, *everyone* wants to win. The real question is *why* do we want to win? And we came up with three things. The first is that we want to win for each other. Because you must admit, it's hard to play selfishly when you're playing for your brothers."

Louis stood and picked up where Austin had left off. "And if we all play for each other, we all benefit."

Around the room, players nodded in agreement as they tapped away on their tablets and laptops.

"The second reason," Louis continued, "is that we want to win for the fans and for the city—to give something back to the people who come out and cheer for us week in and week out."

More heads nodded.

Now Wesley rose and joined his teammates. "And the last one is that we want to inspire all the kids out there who dream of someday sitting right here in this room."

Justin looked over at me and smiled. Truly, it would have been a touching moment had someone not shouted, "Holy cow! He *can* talk!" triggering a chorus of laughter that continued until Joe brought the room back under control. "All right, so that's our *L*—our larger purpose," he recapped. "We want to win for each other, win for the fans, and win to inspire greatness in others."

As I scanned the room, most of the players seemed to be in agreement. They were sitting up straight, nodding, and taking notes. As expected, however, there were a handful—mostly veterans—who slouched back in their chairs, rolling their eyes. The team leaders had won over most of the room, though, and sometimes that's all it takes to launch a movement.

"And it starts this week," Joe stated emphatically. "I've arranged for us to practice on Friday at the local high school just down the road, so even fans who might not be able to come to a regular season game can come out and watch us play."

My eyebrows shot up. *Another good move.* Clearly, Joe had

taken to heart Austin's and Wesley's comments about not being able to afford tickets when they were young. For the past three seasons, the Vipers had opted for closed practices to eliminate as many outside distractions as possible—a direction a lot of teams had taken in recent years. In fact, only a handful still hold their training camps off-site, as most now choose to stay within the confines of their own facilities for that critical monthlong evaluation period. Although that does cut down on distractions and is more cost-effective, I've always thought there are some drawbacks to that approach. I loved going off-site for training camp, even if it meant sleeping in a dorm room. In fact, I think the sacrifice and everyone feeling a bit uncomfortable is a plus. And the open training camp provides a great opportunity for players to not only bond and build camaraderie but also to engage with the community. A practice at an Orlando high school would be a great way to continue building that engagement.

A few groans and disgruntled mumbles rose up. Apparently Joe heard them too, because he quickly called everyone back to order. "And now," he continued, his tone much more serious, "I'd like to address the elephant in the room."

That caught their attention.

"I'm sure by now you've all heard the rumblings about the team's potential relocation to Oakland."

Silence.

"Well, I don't know about you," he began, his voice rising, "but I for one would like to see this franchise stay right here in Orlando!" Joe's emphatic statement was met with a raucous round of applause and shouts of support, from both the players and the rest of the coaching staff.

Joe let the applause go on for a few more seconds and then waved the group down with his arms. "And I can't think of a better way to show our fans and this city how much we want to stay than to bring them home a championship!" The room erupted in applause and spontaneous celebration before Joe even finished the sentence.

There you go, I thought, rising to my feet and clapping along. *That's what unity looks like.*

GOOD SIGNS, BAD SIGNS— WE HAD OUR SHARE

THAT FRIDAY, THE STANDS at nearby Orlando Heights High School were packed, and the entire field was bathed in lime green and black. Perry Richards, head of the Vipers PR department, had done a spectacular job promoting the event, drawing not only thousands of fans to the small high school football field but a slew of media as well.

As a special treat, I had driven up a handful of players from Justin's Little League team to watch the practice, and they were having an absolute blast seeing their favorite players up close and in person, most of them for the first time. From what I could tell, Owen was having a slightly less enjoyable evening, spending most of it surrounded by reporters peppering him with questions about the possible move and the upcoming stadium referendum.

Down on the field, the kickers were alternating field goal attempts against a live rush. Everyone expected the previous year's kicker, Patrick Kingsby, to easily make the roster over the rookie Gym had signed after the draft. Despite a terrific career at Louisiana Tech, the recent grad had gone undrafted. Now his best chance to make a team was to get in some preseason kicks, then wait by the phone in case another team's kicker got injured or shanked one too many times after the season was underway.

"For the last time, I never said we were relocating." Owen's voice carried all the way over to where I was sitting on the edge of the stands, drawing my attention away from the action on the field.

"All I said was that the current facilities are simply not acceptable. The Vipers are a world-class organization. They should have a world-class stadium. Look at Dallas, Atlanta, Tampa Bay, and Minnesota," he continued. "Those teams all have state-of-the-art facilities. If this city wants our franchise to be competitive, that's what it's going to take."

"Yeah, but even *you* have to admit—the current proposal is pretty one-sided." I recognized the voice. It was Harding, the sports columnist for the *Orlando Press* who had skewered Joe earlier that spring. "What you're proposing isn't exactly fan friendly."

"Listen—" Owen's voice had a definite edge to it—"if we had a new stadium, we would be a prime candidate to host the Super Bowl. And as you know, that would bring an awful lot of tourists to the area."

"With all due respect," Harding countered, "Orlando is home to Disney World, Epcot, Universal Studios, and Sea World. We're swimming in tourists."

I had to agree—he'd made a good point. Owen was going to have to change tactics, and quickly. Before he could even open his mouth, however, Harding spoke up again.

"According to this proposal, local organizations aren't even guaranteed use of the new stadium."

"Now, wait a minute!" The edge in Owen's voice intensified. "You guys keep quoting me out of context . . ."

"Tony!" a voice called up from below. When I glanced down, I saw Gym McKenzie waving at me from the track in front of the stands. I waved back, then turned to Justin.

"Hey, buddy, I'm going to go down and talk with Mr. McKenzie for a few minutes. You guys stay put, okay? I'll be right back."

His eyes never even left the field. "Uh-huh."

"Looks like Owen's got his hands full over there," I said when I reached Gym. "To be honest, I'm surprised you even got him here for this."

"Mark told him there would be potential sponsors here tonight," Gym said, smiling.

"Really?" I said with surprise. As far as I knew, sponsors usually didn't show up for this kind of thing.

"Well, if you consider thousands of fans as potential sponsors—" he gestured back toward the stands—"then, yes."

I had to hand it to Mark. "Getting Owen out into the community to interact with the fan base and see how much the team means to the city was a stroke of genius!" I said.

"No," he responded, "getting Perry to send a special invitation to every Cub Scout troop, Little League, and Pop Warner team in a fifty-mile radius was a stroke of genius. Look at all these kids!"

I quickly scanned the area. "These guys will be lucky if they get out of here by midnight with all the autographs they're going to be signing."

"Well, on the upside," Gym pointed out, "there are a lot more guys out there to split up the autographs tonight than there will be in a couple of weeks."

"That's true," I acknowledged, turning my attention to the

field. The rookie kicker had just nailed a fifty-eight-yard attempt with about three yards to spare, drawing a round of applause from the crowd.

"Kid's got a great leg," I said to Gym.

"Yeah, I wish we could keep him." Gym stared wistfully out at the field for a few seconds. "But with a leg like that, I'm sure he'll get picked up somewhere."

When practice wrapped up later, some of the team headed off to the locker room to change, while many players—Austin, Louis, and Wesley included—stayed behind to sign jerseys and footballs for the kids, who were now storming the field.

"Dad!" I turned to see Justin anxiously looking from me to the field, clutching his Quarles jersey in his hand.

I nodded and watched as he and his friends scampered down the stands and over to the field.

"You might be here till midnight yourself," Gym laughed.

"Ha! I might at that."

"Well . . . I should probably go over and save Owen and Perry," Gym said. "You coming by at all next week?"

"I don't think so. I'll be at the Detroit game, though."

"Excellent," he said, shaking my hand. "I'll see you then."

As Gym made his way through the throng of reporters still haranguing Owen, I headed over to the sidelines to talk with Stan. Out of the corner of my eye, I noticed a small pack of kids wearing Ariet jerseys and chasing after the star wide receiver as he headed back up the hill toward the main building. Despite their repeated cries of "Mr. Ariet!" and "Wickie!" and "Will you please sign my jersey?" he didn't even turn around.

Uh-oh. I was pleased to see how many players had stayed behind, but this wasn't good. At all. I noticed Austin watching the scene as well. He simply shook his head and reached for another jersey that had been frantically thrust in front of him.

"Hey, Stan," I said, nodding toward the rookie kicker, "that kid's got quite a leg on him!"

"Yeah," Stan said. "Can you believe that last kick? He could've hit from 60, 61 easy."

"Great work ethic too," I added, watching the young player line up another attempt.

"Yeah," he sighed. "Probably won't keep him, though. Pat's been rock-solid out there, and we don't need two kickers. A good problem to have. I've been with teams that couldn't make a kick."

"Any strong prospects for other positions?" I asked.

Stan took a deep breath and exhaled slowly as he looked at the laminated card he kept in his back pocket. "Several, actually. But it'll all depend on what Whit and DC decide to do."

That was true. Except for the punter and kicker, special teams rarely got a say in final roster decisions.

"Anyone worth fighting for?" I pushed.

He thought for a second. "Maybe one. Pete Ramsey. Amazing punt returner. Unbelievable speed. But again, it all depends on Whit and DC."

"Where are Whit and DC?" I asked, scanning the field.

"I think they headed back up already."

"Joe too?"

"Yep. I was going to head back myself, but I think I'll hang out down here a little while longer and watch this kid kick a few more."

I turned to look at the crowd of kids gathered around Austin, Louis, and the others. Louis and Wesley had pretty much finished up, but Austin was still surrounded. In fact, the circle was two deep in front of Justin and his friends.

"Hey, Stan, since you're staying . . . could I ask you a huge favor?"

"Of course."

"I just want to check in with Joe for a second before he leaves. My son Justin and his friends are over there waiting for Austin to sign their jerseys." I waved at Justin, who waved back. "Could you please keep an eye on them for me? I won't be long."

"Sure thing, Tony. I'd be happy to."

"Thanks, Stan." We both watched as the rookie put another fifty-plus yarder through the goalposts.

"Man, I wish I could keep two," Stan sighed.

•　　•　　•　　•　　•

The Orlando Heights High School locker room made the Vipers' undersized changing area look like the Taj Mahal by comparison. Then again, the sheer size differential between the Vipers players and the average high schooler probably accounted for much of the cramped and chaotic atmosphere.

"Come on, guys, let's pack it up!" Joe announced from the back of the room. "I want everyone back on the buses in fifteen."

I waved Joe down from across the room. He nodded, then pointed off to the left, where the PE teacher's office had been cleared out for Vipers staff.

"Great practice tonight," I said, pulling the door shut behind me. "Austin looks fantastic, and I really like the look of some of those draft picks."

"Thanks, Tony. You know, I think we've got a really good shot to go deep into the playoffs this year." He looked more enthusiastic than I'd ever seen him.

"Definitely," I agreed. "And that was some great fan turnout."

"Yeah. Did you happen to notice Owen out there?" His face broke into a wide smile. "The local media was really letting him have it."

"Yes, they were," I agreed. "I think that's good. It might help him see firsthand how his decisions are being perceived by the community. A lot of things look great on paper, but when you stop to consider how they're impacting the people involved . . ."

Joe nodded. "I guess we just have to hope Owen finds his SOUL before the voters make their voices heard come February."

"That *would* help," I agreed.

Suddenly Joe's smile faded, and his expression took on a more serious cast.

"Listen, Tony. I know I came off kind of rough when you first came on board. I just want to apologize and tell you how much I really do appreciate what you're doing."

Wow. I hadn't expected that.

"Thanks, Joe. That means a lot. And I meant what I said that day. You are a fantastic coach, and you've got a lot of talent on this team and a lot of great people in this organization. Give Owen a little time. In fact, give everyone a little time. The SOUL principles *will* work. I've seen it. But you're not going to get 100 percent buy-in right off the bat. Just stay the course, stick to the principles, and it'll come together."

Joe looked at me and sighed. "I hope so."

We walked out of the office just in time to see a very frustrated Austin Quarles, still in his pads and practice jersey, storm into the locker room. After a quick scan, his eyes settled on Wickie Ariet, fully dressed, who was sitting in front of a locker, eyes closed and earbuds in, listening to music on his phone.

"Hey, Wickie," Austin barked, making a beeline over to his teammate. Wickie pulled out his earbuds and shot a surprised look at Austin, who was now standing right in front of him.

"You know you blew off a bunch of kids out there," Austin said.

"Hey," replied Wickie with a shrug as he leaned back against the locker, "it's bad enough I gotta stay in a dorm when I live less than five miles from the stadium. I'm not standing around some Podunk high school field on a Friday night signing autographs for a bunch of kids."

Austin's eyes could have bored a hole straight through Wickie's skull.

"You don't get it, do you?" said Austin. "You didn't just blow off the kids; you blew off your teammates."

"What are you talking about?" Wickie shot back, now standing up inches from Austin.

"It's always the same guys out there after every game signing autographs, while you just head for the showers. We're supposed to be a team here, Wickie. What one of us does, all of us do—and that includes you." By this point several other players had stopped what they were doing to listen in.

"Should I step in here?" Joe asked me in a low voice.

I just shook my head. I'd heard Peyton Manning give this same lecture many times in Indy.

"No," I said, holding my hand up in front of him. "Trust me, it'll mean a lot more coming from Austin."

And apparently Louis.

"Austin's right," the outspoken linebacker added, turning to face the rest of the players milling around the room. "In case you missed it earlier this week, this is exactly what we were talking about—not being selfish, owning your role on this team—" he turned to face Wickie—"on and off the field." The room was suddenly quiet.

"And showing all those kids out there what a real pro football player looks like," Austin added.

"This team supports each other, and we support our community," Louis picked up, addressing the entire locker room. "You either get on board with that—"

"Or what?" Wickie said, leaning forward into Austin.

"Or you'll be answering to me." Every head in the room turned to face Joe, who paused briefly to let the weight of his comment sink in.

"All right," Joe continued, "show's over. I want everyone on the buses in five."

The locker room became a flurry of activity as players scrambled to gather up their gear. Joe turned to me and said, "Sorry, Tony. I just felt like I had to say something."

"Hey, it's your team, Joe. Your call. And you did the right thing," I assured him. "Like I said, just stay the course. They'll get there."

After slamming his locker shut, Wickie stormed out.

Just then Gym walked into the room, a puzzled look on his face. "Hey, did I miss something?"

Joe glanced at Gym and said, "Oh, nothing much. The guys just put Wickie in his place."

Gym's eyes grew wide. "Wow! I'd have paid to see that."

"Don't worry, Gym," Joe sighed. "I have a feeling it won't be the last time."

ONE BLOCK SHORT

THREE WEEKS LATER, I was sitting in the third row of the coaches booth at Ford Field in Detroit, watching the Vipers' third preseason game, which traditionally serves as a dress rehearsal for the first regular-season game. Teams tend to play their projected starters for a longer period, often the entire first half, to give them a chance to work at game speeds and in game conditions—but still have two weeks to recover from any minor injuries that might occur before the start of the regular season. I had decided to stay off the headsets. I didn't want to overstep my boundaries since I wasn't part of the game planning and didn't really have a role other than giving Joe my thoughts on how the starters looked.

What I could see down on the field was a clear improvement over the first two weeks of preseason. The offense was moving the ball fairly well. Austin had led a first solid drive, completing three passes to Wickie, and Don was running hard and gaining good chunks of yardage.

The defense held the Lions on their first possession, and

with the Vipers up 7–0, Wesley was in to field the upcoming punt.

The punt was long and high, and Wesley drifted back for it, never turning his hips to get back to the spot he thought it would land.

That'll come with experience, I thought.

Wesley kept drifting until finally he attempted to reach back and make the catch over his right shoulder at his own 6 yard line. Sure enough, the ball bounced off his fingertips, and his white jersey disappeared into a sea of Honolulu blue in a scramble for the fumble. Moments later, the referees unpiled the players and signaled that the Lions had, in fact, recovered the fumble—in the end zone.

Touchdown, Lions.

Ouch. That's not going to sit well with Stan or Joe.

When the offense got the ball back, Austin completed a quick slant to the slot receiver. Then Don picked up twelve yards on an outside run. After another run for no gain, Whit called for a Double Right, Scat Left, 548 H-under. In layman's terms, that meant Wickie would make a break for the post, while Don hung back to block against a possible pass rush from the right.

Austin took the snap, followed by a five-step dropback while Wickie ran his route, but before he could release the pass, the blitzing linebacker came around the right side untouched and clobbered Austin with a vicious but clean hit to his chest.

Oh, man. I sat back in my chair.

Despite having a fantastic view of the blitzing linebacker, Don had just waved at his opponent like a matador instead of stepping in and blocking like he was supposed to.

For a moment, I thought Whit was going to break right through the glass, charge down onto the field, and throttle Don personally. In fact, all the coaches were animated and upset. Then suddenly everyone went quiet, their eyes glued to the field, where the quarterback was still lying on his back, his left hand clutching his throwing shoulder.

"Oh, no. Not again," Whit moaned.

"Get Brendan up," the quarterbacks coach said into his headset.

Down on the sidelines, backup quarterback Brendan Quinlan pulled on his helmet and quickly started throwing warm-up passes while the trainers helped Austin off the field and into the locker room for X-rays and an exam by the team's orthopedist.

Brendan finished out the rest of the quarter, as Austin's day was done. The first-team offense sputtered, and backups came in for the second half. The backups, most of whom were destined to be released anyway, played well. Other than a dropped pass by Wesley Robinson late in the fourth quarter, nothing else of note happened.

Although the Vipers won 30–20, I knew the flight back would be subdued until we had a more detailed report on Austin's shoulder.

Ahhhh . . . preseason.

• • • • •

We didn't get back from Detroit until 3 a.m., so I opted to stay in Orlando that night. Before making the trek home late the next morning, I met with Gym, Joe, and the offensive coaches. By then the video staff had created film showing the game from two camera angles—one shot from the top of the stadium at the 50 yard line, the other from high in one end zone. (Fans usually prefer the 50-yard-line view—the side view—similar to what they see on television, but the end zone angle is often of greatest help to coaches, especially in seeing holes develop in a play.) We watched each play twice in succession, once from each angle. Either perspective, however, was enough to confirm the lack of effort on Don's "block."

On the upside, Austin's X-rays showed no evidence of a fracture, and the MRI didn't show any structural damage, so barring any further issues—which Joe planned to avoid by having him sit out the final preseason game—Austin would be ready to play on opening day against the Cardinals.

Needless to say, Joe and Whit were both furious that Don had blown such an easy block.

"Did you talk to Don after the game?" Gym asked Joe after the film session.

"He said it *wasn't his job*," Joe seethed, punctuating the last three words.

"Wasn't his job?" Gym echoed in shock. "Then whose job was it? He was the only back in the game!"

Joe shook his head. "He knows that. He said he wasn't going to risk getting hurt blocking a linebacker—especially in a preseason game."

A vein in Joe's neck was starting to throb, so Whit jumped in. "He said he's too valuable as a running back to be used as a blocker, and that if we're going to be passing, we should either put one of the other running backs in or design the protection so he doesn't have to block."

Now Whit's neck was sporting a vein of its own.

"He realizes that doesn't make any sense, right?" I asked. "I mean, if you're going to pull Don every time you decide to pass, you might as well wave a flag to the other teams that you're throwing it."

"Exactly!" Joe and Whit shot back in unison.

"Other thoughts, Tony?" asked Gym.

I shook my head in disbelief. "Coach Noll never had to take Franco Harris out because he was unwilling to block. The same with Edgerrin James when I was coaching the Colts. Even Warrick Dunn, who was always one of the smallest players in the league, would throw his body in the way to protect our quarterbacks in Tampa. Bottom line, the role of a *complete* running back includes pass protection, and Don is a complete running back. Or he should be. He needs to own that role."

"What should we do?" asked Joe. "Bench him? Suspend him?"

"We might be on thin ice trying to suspend him for this," Gym said. "I think we'd have to either bench him . . . or cut him."

Joe and Whit exchanged panicked glances.

"We can't cut him," Joe blurted out.

"Losing Don would be a huge blow to our offense," added Whit.

"Well, we can't have Austin running for his life all season," Gym pointed out.

"I agree," I said. "When the star quarterback is hurt because a teammate refuses to protect him, you have to respond."

"So what do we do?" Whit asked.

Suddenly everyone's eyes were fixed on me. *I told them this wouldn't be easy.* Actually, of the four of us, mine was the easiest decision.

"That's something you guys are going to have to decide," I said as three sets of shoulders slumped in disappointment.

After staring at the floor for almost a full minute, Joe took off his hat and sighed. "Let me talk to him again. Give him one more chance to own his role. At the same time, it might help if we show Don that we understand his concern about getting injured himself. Whit, could you and your position coaches come up with a blocking scheme to help Don minimize the risks of becoming injured himself?"

"Will do. But what if Don doesn't budge and refuses to block?" Whit asked.

I decided to toss out one last piece of advice. "You know, Coach Noll used to have a saying: 'Every player is important . . . but *no one* is indispensable.'"

"Try telling that to Don," said Gym.

"Actually," I suggested, "you might want to think about telling that to all of them."

Silence.

Like I said, it wasn't going to be easy.

GIVE-AND-TAKE

THE NEXT EIGHT DAYS PASSED WITHOUT MUCH DRAMA. Camp had broken, and players had either gone back to their homes in Orlando or moved into hotels to wait out the final cuts. The Vipers were still carrying eighty-five guys on the roster, having released only a handful following the third preseason game, including the rookie kicker who had nailed the fifty-eight yarder a few weeks back. Stan was sorry to see him go, but he, Gym, and Joe had agreed that releasing him early was the best way for the kid to possibly find a permanent team.

All around the draft room, whiteboards were covered with names, salaries, cap numbers, and positions. The OVERALL board had been transformed to a FINAL 53 board, where magnets with forty-nine names were currently grouped by position. As usual, deciding on the final four names was proving quite challenging.

Based on what Joe and Gym had decided as the "optimal" roster construction, the Vipers still needed a fifth wide receiver, a sixth linebacker, and another offensive and defensive lineman.

However, if they kept Pete Ramsey, a player whose only contributions would come as a punt returner, one of those four other positions would have to go a man short to start the season.

From where I sat, Wesley Robinson was the key to the debate. However, Whit simply didn't trust him, which was understandable. Wesley was still running the wrong routes from time to time, which wasn't uncommon for a rookie, but Whit was also displeased with his two dropped balls in that third preseason game at Detroit—one as a receiver and one as a punt returner.

"I just don't trust him at receiver," Whit said. "I'd rather keep Hamilton as the fifth receiver." Hamilton Nobles was a ten-year veteran who had definitely lost a step over time, but he was still a solid receiver who knew the system and got all the routes. His ceiling was limited, but he wouldn't have the growing pains of Wesley.

However, Wesley's rookie salary was much lower than Hamilton's. If the Vipers kept Hamilton, they couldn't afford Larry Bannister, a veteran linebacker, and would have to keep a younger, less expensive, less experienced player at that position.

Gym jumped in. "DC, tell us about the two linebackers. Can you play with either on the roster?"

"I'd prefer Larry," DC admitted, "but I could live with either linebacker, especially if we can keep another defensive lineman. I just don't feel like we can give up either of the defensive roster slots, so if we keep the return-only guy, I would prefer he take one of the slots that was set aside for an offensive player. If not, we'll make do."

Joe spoke up. "Wilson, tell us about the two wide receivers. If it were your call, what would you do with that fifth receiver roster spot?"

Wilson, the wide receivers coach, glanced over at Whit, then spoke. "Well, I agree with Whit. I like Wesley—I really do. He's a natural leader, and he's got a great work ethic. He's like a sponge, watching film and working on his own, but it's just hard to trust him right now. Too many rookie mistakes. Hamilton might cost a little more, but at least with him we know what we're getting—at least in week one, which is right around the corner."

I watched the discussion with interest. It was almost identical to the debate we'd had in Tampa over Ronde Barber, a third-round pick out of Virginia. Ronde hadn't played very well in training camp, and Monte Kiffin, our defensive coordinator, and some of our defensive coaches wanted to cut him in favor of a veteran player. But like Wesley, Ronde was a natural leader who had a fantastic work ethic. We knew he would get better, and in the end we all agreed to keep him.

But that is part of the healthy dynamic between the assistant coaches, who are looking at selecting the best players to win right now, and the head coach and general manager, who are looking at developing the best team for the future as well. Monte was right in that Ronde wasn't quite ready that first year, and he didn't play in many games. But by his second year, we knew we had something special in him. Ronde went on to play for sixteen years and went to five Pro Bowls. He will probably end up in the Hall of Fame.

We had teased Monte over the years for wanting to cut Ronde, but it was actually a great lesson for us. Sometimes you have to be patient with young players, and you always have to look at the long-term potential of the players when making roster decisions.

As I listened to the exchange over Wesley, I was especially impressed as I considered how far Whit and DC had come in just a few months. They were both passionately pleading their cases, but they weren't bludgeoning each other the way they had in the spring. There was almost a genuine sense of unity in the room. I sensed just one thing was missing.

Gym looked at me. "Tony, what do you think?"

"I think we should take a break and step away from this for a few minutes—give everyone a chance to digest what they've heard."

Gym nodded in agreement. "All right, everyone. Let's be back in five."

As people began milling about the room, I caught up to Stan, who'd stepped into the hallway.

"Hey, Stan, I was just wondering . . . what's your opinion on all this? You were pretty high on Pete Ramsey during camp. You still want him?"

Stan thought for a moment and sighed. "Actually, I think there might be more of an upside to keeping Wesley."

"Then why don't you say something?"

He hedged a little, then said, "I don't want to get anyone worked up, especially with Whit and DC actually getting along right now."

"I get that," I admitted. "But your job here is to help the special teams be as strong as they can be. Remember our discussion about everybody owning their role? You need to own *that*. If you've got an opinion, you need to share it. You're a part of this team too. Unity isn't just about everyone getting along; it's also about making sure everyone feels they're included, valued, and contributing to the larger purpose."

Stan took a deep breath. "All right," he conceded. "But they've never actually gotten along before."

"Now's not before, though, is it?" I responded with a smile.

•　　•　　•　　•　　•

As everyone settled back into the draft room, I sidled up to Gym and whispered, "Why don't you see what Stan thinks about this one?" He looked at me in surprise and then glanced over at Stan, who was sitting quietly at the far edge of the table. When Gym looked back at me, I just nodded.

"Okay, everyone," Gym announced, quieting the room. "We've got four spots to go here, so let's get back at it." Before anyone else could speak up, he leaned forward and looked down the table to his left. "Stan, you've spent a lot of time working with Pete Ramsey and Wesley Robinson. What do you think?"

A soft murmur rose up in the room, followed by silence as all eyes turned to Stan.

Stan cast a quick glance in my direction, then took a deep breath and began.

"They're both solid, but Wesley has a little more burst, which gives him a better chance to break a big return."

"But what about Wesley's dropped punt in Detroit?" asked Whit.

Stan shook his head. "That was bad. But listen, I've seen him make that catch countless times in practice. The game will slow down for him the more action he sees and the more Wilson works with him. He's already putting in a ton of extra time watching film and studying the playbook. Yes, he's making a lot of rookie mistakes, but he's got great potential, not only as a return man but as a receiver too."

"So," Gym interjected, "you think we should keep Wesley instead of Pete?"

Stan thought for a second. "Yes."

"Pete's got some pretty wicked speed," Whit chimed in from the other end of the table. "You sure Wesley is better?"

"Listen," Stan continued, "don't get me wrong. I'd love to have Pete's speed on my return team." He paused before continuing. "But we'll be a lot better on special teams with the veteran linebacker, Larry, instead of the younger one. Wesley's salary allows DC to keep Larry and still be under the cap. So

DC gets to shore up his defense, I get a solid return guy with an unlimited upside and also a veteran linebacker solid on special teams, and in another year or so, Whit and Wilson will likely have themselves an outstanding wide receiver. To me, it's a win-win-win."

The room went silent for a moment while everyone processed what had just transpired. Finally, Gym turned to Whit.

"Whit, can you live with that?"

Before Whit could respond, Wilson jumped in.

"I'll get him there, Whit. Maybe not in time for the Cardinals in two weeks, but I'll get him there."

Whit looked over at Joe, who nodded reassuringly.

"Okay," Whit said. "Let's give the kid a shot."

I smiled at Stan across the table, then pointed at him and mouthed, "You."

He shook his head, smiled, and using his thumbs and index fingers, made the letter *U*.

GAINS AND LOSSES

I'D LIKE TO SAY that the first four regular season games showed the brilliance of keeping Wesley Robinson on the roster, but in his limited amount of time on the field, he managed to muff an opening kickoff, drop two passes, and run the wrong route on a crucial third and long.

I followed up with Stan and Wilson by phone, and both remained cautiously optimistic, pointing out that the rookie had been working his tail off at practice every week and, other than Austin, was putting in more time watching film than anyone else on the roster.

Whit and Joe were quickly losing patience, though. Had the Vipers not gotten off to a strong 3–1 start and all of Wesley's mistakes not come during wins, I think his fate might have been sealed early on.

In week five, the Vipers took on the Texans in Houston, where Whit had served as an assistant coach before coming to Orlando. I opted to stay home with my four youngest boys—Justin, Jason, Jalen, and Jaden—and watch the game from the comfort of our family room.

The Vipers started off strong, controlling the line of scrimmage on both offense and defense. Both Don and Austin were playing well, and the balanced running and passing attack kept the Texans offense on the bench for much of the game.

After Louis Blackstock intercepted a pass and returned it for a touchdown midway through the fourth quarter, we went up 24–21, and it looked like we would improve to 4–1 on the season.

With 2:30 left in the game, our defense stopped the Texans at their own 35, setting up a fourth and three. With no time-outs left, the Texans decided to punt, hoping to pin us deep in our own territory. That would at least give them a shot at getting the ball back with a few seconds on the clock so they could attempt a tying field goal.

On the kick, their punter didn't get as much of the ball as he wanted, and Wesley was able to make a fair catch at the Vipers' own 20. All Austin needed to do to win the game was hand the ball off to Don a couple of times, keep the ball in bounds, and make one first down. So I was stunned when Whit called three straight pass plays—all deep balls, and all incomplete, forcing us to punt with 1:17 left on the clock.

The Texans effectively worked the sidelines, stopping the clock after several solid gains. Then a simple screen pass, intended to put them in field goal position, turned into a thirty-eight-yard scamper into the end zone, putting Houston up 28–24 with just six seconds left—much to the delight of the home crowd and the chagrin of the Dungy household.

When time expired, the boys and I watched as Joe Webster walked across the field to shake hands with the opposing coach, his face a peculiar mix of disappointment, anger, and confusion. I was still trying to process what had just happened myself when

Justin turned to me, shook his head, and said, "Now *that* is going to be one long flight home."

It certainly is.

•　　•　　•　　•　　•

I could hear the shouting as soon as I entered the stadium on Monday. I followed the noise all the way to the offensive meeting room, where Joe and Gym were holding Whit and DC apart. Joe was trying to subdue an indignant Whit, and Gym had taken on the red-faced DC.

"Whoa!" I called out, stepping into the mix. "Let's all take it easy here, gentlemen."

For a second, the two coordinators stopped shouting at each other and eased up on their attacks, allowing Joe and Gym to stand down.

"That's better. Now why doesn't everyone go back to their corners." I was trying to lighten the mood a bit, but the stern expressions on Whit's and DC's faces told me it was going to take a lot more than a simple boxing joke to restore the peace.

"What's the problem?" I asked, though I was pretty sure I knew.

DC spoke—or should I say, shouted—first.

"This . . . this . . . guy—" he stammered, barely able to get the words out—"we had that game won! All he had to do was run the ball. Even if we wouldn't have made a first down, the Texans would have been left with only about twenty seconds. But no, he's got to show off in front of his former team and try to run up the score! Heaven forbid we win by only three. We lost that game for one reason and one reason alone: Whit's ego!"

"What we saw yesterday," Whit shouted back, "was another blown lead by our defense! How do you give up a thirty-eight-yard touchdown on a simple screen pass?"

"There wouldn't even have been a screen pass if you—"

"All right, enough!" Joe broke in. "I had too much of this on the plane. Now both of you—" he gestured to chairs at opposite ends of the table—"sit down."

"Whit," Joe began, his voice calm, measured, "I know what it's like to play a former team." Whit opened his mouth to speak, but Joe quickly held up his hand to silence him. "But if you want full rein to call this offense, I need to know I can trust you to do what's best for *the team*—not what's best for you."

Hmm. Well-handled, Joe. I looked across the table at Gym, who nodded in appreciation of the normally fiery coach's more restrained approach.

Even Whit had calmed down—until he looked across the table and saw DC sitting there, arms crossed and gloating.

"You want to talk about doing what's best for the team," Whit challenged, pointing at DC, "then tell this guy it's not okay to take the defense out for private dinners and excursions after practices."

"What?" Gym and Joe simultaneously blurted, heads whipping around to face the now-scowling DC.

"You can't take the defense on special outings, DC," Joe reprimanded him. "What were you thinking?"

DC looked incredulous. "Seriously? Over the past three seasons, we've taken the entire team on trips to theme parks, to Orlando Magic games, and to play paintball. All I did was take my guys out for pizza and bowling after the Kansas City game to celebrate the win. It was probably the cheapest outing we've ever done here."

"The money's not the point, DC," Gym pointed out. "All of those other trips were for the whole team—not just one unit."

"Yeah, but my guys played great in that game, yet all the media coverage focused on Austin, Wickie, and Don. My guys are always getting overlooked in favor of his," he sneered, gesturing toward Whit.

Joe looked discouraged. With a few minor exceptions, everything had been going remarkably well this season, and now one loss and Whit and DC were right back at each other's throats. I thought about saying something but then decided to hold off. This was Joe's team, and the way he handled getting his two top assistants on the same page would go a long way in determining how this season would play out.

Joe stared at DC for a few seconds, then at Whit, and then at me. I gave him a subtle nod of encouragement.

Stick to the principles, Joe.

Joe took a deep breath and slowly exhaled. "All right, let's get one thing straight right now—" he subtly shifted his head from one side to the other—"there are no *my guys*, *your guys*, or *his guys* on this roster. We are a team. We win as a team, and we lose as a team.

"And when we win," he said, looking straight at DC, "we celebrate as a team. The team always comes first," he added, zeroing in on Whit. "*Always.*"

The room was silent. Whit and DC just stared at each other. I wasn't anticipating any hugs or high fives, but Joe's speech had been effective. Both men had calmed down considerably.

"Okay, then," Joe said, pushing his chair back and rising to his feet. "Let's get ready for Atlanta."

Whit and DC rose and headed toward the door. Neither said anything to the other, but both gave slight nods to Joe as they left.

As the three men headed off down the hall, Gym turned to me. "So what do you think?"

"Honestly?"

"Of course," Gym replied.

"I think you may have gained more from this loss than if you'd won the game."

Gym nodded. "I think you may be right."

A Giant Problem

In the weeks since the blowup, both Whit and DC had completely come around and embraced Joe's message of unity. Stunningly, Whit even went to DC and privately apologized, not only for the confrontation but also for his questionable play calling at the end of the game.

And it was a good thing everyone was getting along, because over the next three weeks, the Vipers won only once. Immediately following the Houston debacle, we lost to the Falcons 30–6, having played poorly on both sides of the ball. Stan's special teams were the lone bright spot in the game plan, with Patrick Kingsby hitting two field goals over fifty yards in the third quarter.

The coaches and players put their poor performance behind them the following week, snapping their two-game losing streak with a road win over Washington. Then they dropped a close game the next week to the Jaguars.

With the team sitting at 4–4 halfway through the regular season, the media were all writing pieces about the "same old

Vipers," which Joe wisely used as a motivational tool to keep the team focused and determined heading into week nine to face the Giants.

This was my first road trip of the regular season, and though I loved listening in on the coordinators' discussions, I opted to sit with Terry and Owen in the visiting owners box. Not only had it been a while since I'd touched base with either of them, but frankly, the food in the owners box was always much better than in the coaches booth.

For a while, the game was better too.

Whit was calling a brilliant game. He'd run a trick play in the first quarter that had gone for a touchdown and had been mixing run and pass plays in a way that kept the Giants' pass rush on their heels. With time in the pocket, Austin had completed a number of downfield passes, and Don was running well.

That all changed after halftime.

Early in the third quarter, with the Vipers leading 17–7, Austin dropped back to pass and was blindsided by a Giants rusher who came unblocked from the left side of the formation and absolutely leveled the Pro Bowl quarterback. On the upside, Austin had somehow managed to hold on to the ball.

Unfortunately, he wasn't able to hold on to his faculties. As two Vipers trainers helped Austin stagger to the sideline, it was clear even from where I was sitting that he was in bad shape.

"*What* was Don thinking on that play?" Owen shouted. "He all but stepped out of the way and pointed the rusher in Austin's direction!"

I hated to admit it, but Owen wasn't that far off. The Giants linebacker hadn't even done a good job of disguising his blitz. Don knew his assignment; he just didn't do it.

Minutes later, Gym poked his head into the owners box

and confirmed what I already suspected: Austin had suffered a concussion and wouldn't be returning to the field.

Brendan Quinlan took a few quick practice snaps on the sideline before going in to replace Austin. Without the starting quarterback, however, the second half was a disaster. Three false starts, two sacks, and two interceptions resulted in a final score of 24–17, Giants. You could have heard a pin drop on the plane ride home.

•   •   •   •   •

The mood remained somber when I arrived at the stadium the following day. The couple of staffers I passed said hello politely, but none stopped to chat. Before heading to my office, I decided to see how Joe was holding up. His door was open as I approached. A scowling Don Buerkle sat in front of Joe's desk, with Whit standing next to him, arms crossed. Not wanting to interrupt, I took a step back. Joe, however, had seen me and motioned me inside.

"Are you kidding me?" Don said to Joe as I entered. He sat motionless in his chair, still in his street clothes. Whit had been so angry that morning, I later learned, that he'd met the veteran running back in the parking lot and ushered him directly to Joe's office.

"I've rushed for over one hundred yards seven times already this year. I'm second in overall yards in the league!" he said, his face a mask of disbelief.

"But no matter how many times we talk to you about it, you still refuse to block on pass plays," Joe stated calmly, but with a decided edge to his voice. "And now thanks to you, we've lost our starting quarterback for at least the next two weeks, maybe longer. I'm tired of talking."

"So that's it. I'm out against Green Bay next week," Don stated flatly, his eyes still searching Joe's for answers.

"Yes, Don. I'm sitting you down. You'll be inactive this week." To Don's amazement, Joe wasn't wavering. Once again, you could have heard a pin drop. Then Don pushed his chair back, uttered something I couldn't quite make out, and made a beeline for the door.

"You're going to regret this," he said, turning back toward Joe and pointing at him. "Without Austin, I'm the only chance you've got against Green Bay."

Joe just stared him back down. "If that turns out to be true, then you've *really* let your teammates down, haven't you?"

Don quickly searched the room for support, but finding none, burst into the hallway, slamming the door behind him.

Joe threw his hands up.

"You did the right thing, Joe," I said. "He's got to own that role. This is already the second time this year that Austin's gotten hurt because Don refused to block. You were right to call him out on that, and I think you're right to have him sit out Sunday. He's got to learn that his lack of effort is hurting this team more than his talent is helping it."

"Tony's right, Joe," Whit chimed in.

Now it was my turn to be stunned. Whit was on board with benching Don? *Not where I thought he'd be on this . . .*

"He's got to learn. It's not just Austin. Brendan got pasted twice yesterday on blown pass blocking," Whit continued.

"We'll be lucky if that kid doesn't end up getting carried out of Lambeau on a stretcher," sighed Gym.

The room went quiet as all three men tried to decide what to do.

Finally Joe spoke up. "Whit, can you put in a little extra

time with Thomas Dorr this week to make sure he's ready to go in Don's place?"

Whit nodded. "Done. Yes, he and Brendan will be getting a lot of reps this week. We're not gonna beat Green Bay on the ground—especially without Don."

Joe was starting to look a little green.

Whit must have noticed it too. "Don't worry, Joe," he said, clapping the head coach on the shoulder. "We'll be ready."

•　　•　　•　　•　　•

The following Sunday, the Vipers shocked Don—and the league—by going to Green Bay and beating the first-place Packers, 23–21. Brendan Quinlan didn't do anything amazing, but he played a steady, solid game, hitting Wesley for six short passes, and Wickie on a third and long for a touchdown with three minutes left in the fourth quarter. Then Louis came up with an interception to seal the win. Once again, the kids and I had watched from home. Lauren even joined us for the final quarter.

"Is that the one you were telling me about?" she asked when Wesley made a nice over-the-shoulder grab late in the game.

"Yes. He's really coming along."

Of course, it didn't hurt that Wesley had stayed late each night running extra routes with Brendan. The two of them had really developed a nice chemistry. Whit told me he'd even seen Wickie give Wesley a couple of pointers. Apparently, his work ethic had earned the rookie a little respect.

Shortly after I arrived at the stadium the next day, Gym stopped by and asked me to follow him to Joe's office. Along the way, he told me Don had done little the previous week except mope around the stadium; he'd even refused to help get his backup ready for Green Bay. As a result, Joe had decided to sit him another week.

When we arrived, Terry and Whit were already sitting across from the head coach. "You're sitting Don against Tampa?" Terry asked as Gym and I took our places against the wall. "We already dodged a bullet against Green Bay, but . . . Tampa Bay? Isn't that a little risky?"

Terry was right. In addition to this being a huge rivalry game, Tampa Bay was in second place in the division at 6–4, while the Falcons were in first at 7–3. The Falcons had already beaten us, and if we were to lose to Tampa, we could be three games back with only five more to play. At best, the Vipers would be left looking for a wild card berth to get into the playoffs. And even that wouldn't be easy, as there were several teams vying for only two wild card spots.

"Joe, I appreciate what you're trying to do here—I really do," Terry continued. "But we've been doing everything we can to win the fan base over in advance of that referendum in February—ad campaigns, personal appearances, free-ticket giveaways, jersey day, even buy-one-get-one loaded nacho platters. Sitting one of our best players—as a healthy scratch, no less—on a Sunday night game against our biggest rival while we're barely hanging on in the wild card race makes no sense whatsoever!"

To his credit, Joe remained perfectly calm. He quietly said, "I'm sorry, Terry, but my mind is made up. It might not be the best way to beat Tampa, but it's what's best for our *team*."

Tapping his fingers on the leather portfolio he was holding, Terry looked down. I could tell he was feeling conflicted. He really did believe in what we were trying to do, but I suspected he was also taking a lot of heat from Owen on this one.

"Okay," Terry sighed.

Whit jumped in. "I've got the answer. The Dolphins are waiving Fred Ashford today. A friend of mine in Miami called last night and said he wasn't a good fit for them."

Joe's mouth dropped open, as did Terry's and Gym's.

Whit quickly held up his hand before any of them could object. "Before you say anything, yes—my friend told me that Ashford had been complaining about the number of passes he'd been getting. *But* . . . he said that *isn't* the reason they're getting rid of him."

"So why are they letting him go?" asked Gym.

Whit turned to face Gym and Terry. "They don't think they can make the playoffs, so they're focusing on developing the rookies for next season."

I had to admit, the whole thing sounded a little suspect to me, and judging by the looks on the others' faces, they weren't convinced either.

Whit turned back to Joe, his ally in the spring on Ashford. "Joe, listen to me. Austin is still in concussion protocol, and now you're sitting Don. If we pair Fred Ashford up with Wickie, we might at least have a chance of winning this thing."

The room was silent, then Whit continued. "If you decide to do it, Joe, I can handle him. If he complains, I'll deal with it."

Joe shook his head. "No. I've just benched one of my best players for playing selfishly and not owning his role. And strangely enough, I think it's actually unified the rest of the team."

Gym leaned toward me and whispered, "You know, I hadn't thought about it until now, but he's right."

"So how can I replace him with a guy whose reputation for selfish play is practically legendary?" Joe paused for a second to let his point set in. "The answer is, I can't. Not with any integrity. And not without undoing everything we've worked so hard to do here."

Wow. It was hard to believe this was the same guy who lobbied so vigorously to sign Ashford six months ago. I couldn't have been prouder of Joe. Standing up for your principles can be challenging under any circumstances, but to potentially put your career on the line? Now that takes *soul.*

"You'll tell Owen?" Joe said to Terry, knowing that the owner would be interested in the star receiver when he got the news of his release.

Terry chuckled. "I'll tell him," he said, heading out the door.

"Oh, and Terry?" Joe called after him. "Tell him to keep an eye on Wesley Robinson this week. That kid's starting to give Wickie a run for his money!"

Once again, Gym leaned over and whispered, "I think he's right about that, too."

Things were starting to get interesting.

RIVALS

I DROVE UP TO ORLANDO on Thursday afternoon to watch the team practice. There's always an air of extra excitement surrounding a rivalry game, but add in playing at home—on *Sunday Night Football* no less—and you could practically feel the electricity coursing through Serpent World's Viper Pit Stadium.

As it turned out, Joe *was* right—Wesley looked fantastic. All the extra time he'd been putting in helping Brendan get ready over the past two weeks had really paid off. His routes were crisper, and he was coming off the ball faster and playing with much more confidence. He even caught two deep, over-the-shoulder passes without breaking stride.

Brendan was also much improved. He still lacked Austin's accuracy and overall arm strength, but he was getting rid of the ball a lot faster than when he had come off the bench against the Giants.

"They're looking pretty good out there," I said, coming up alongside Whit.

"You know . . . they really are." He sounded almost surprised.

"Is that Austin out there?" I asked, shading my eyes from the sun. It looked like the quarterback was standing near the huddle, dressed more like a coach than a player.

"Yeah. Technically, he's still in concussion protocol, so he can't practice, but he's also faced Tampa's pass rush four or five times, and he wanted to do whatever he could to help Brendan out. I told him he could stay for an hour, but not one minute longer."

"Good move," I said. I was just about to ask how Austin's latest neurological tests had gone when something downfield caught my eye.

"Am I seeing what I think I'm seeing over there?" I asked Whit. He looked up from his clipboard for a second, then nodded and stifled a laugh.

"Yep. Wickie's been trying to teach the kid his 'swim move' so he can get off the line faster."

Joe had told me that Wickie had been giving Wesley some pointers, but somehow seeing it with my own eyes was even more unbelievable. Maybe watching Don ride the bench two weeks in a row made Wickie realize that Joe wasn't kidding when he said *get on board or else*. Or maybe he figured helping Wesley become more of a deep threat might pull some of the double coverage off *himself.* Maybe he just liked the kid. Wesley was definitely popular. Everyone on the team liked him, which—now that I thought about it—was more than I could say for Wickie. It's ironic. As a coach, you always hope the veterans will set a good example for the rookies—show them what being a pro looks like. Of course, sometimes it goes the other way.

"You know, I hate to jinx it," Whit said, looking up from his clipboard again, "but we might actually be okay without Don this week."

"Speaking of Don," I hedged, "any movement there?"

"Well, he's here," Whit sighed, pointing about fifteen yards downfield to where the veteran running back was taking a knee on the sidelines. "I haven't really given him many practice snaps, though. I'm still trying to get Thomas ready. Tampa's got a nasty pass rush. We can't afford to lose Brendan, too."

That's for sure.

I stood off to the side to watch the final hour of practice.

As usual, the kickers closed out the session, with Patrick Kingsby uncharacteristically pulling three straight field goal attempts to the left from fifty yards out.

Well, let's hope it doesn't come down to that *on Sunday.*

As most of the players headed for the showers, Brendan, Wesley, Wickie, Louis, Thomas, and a handful of offensive and defensive linemen stayed out on the field to run a few pass plays against Tampa's blitzes. Brendan managed to get the ball out on time twice, but then he got tagged three straight times from the left. Of course, because it was practice, the rusher merely tapped Brendan's jersey. But come Sunday, Brendan would be facing much worse if Thomas couldn't stop the rush.

"Hey, Coach," Austin said as he walked over toward me.

"Hey, Austin, I thought you'd left. How are you feeling?"

"I'm doing good. Doc would have cleared me for this week, but he told me he wants to be absolutely sure I've recovered."

"That's a wise decision," I said.

We turned back to the field just in time to see Brendan get tagged from the left once again. Austin flinched. I couldn't blame him.

"Thomas is trying," he said, shaking his head. And he was right. This wasn't a case of a running back dodging a block. We'd all seen our fair share of that. "It's almost like he's tripping over his own feet."

Suddenly a voice barked from the sidelines. "Hey, Thomas!" It was Don, still in his pads and carrying his helmet out to the center of the field, where his backup was staring at the ground in frustration. "You're trying to block with your hands. That's why he keeps knocking you off-center. You gotta square up your hips. Take him head-on. You don't have to knock him down—just get in his way. Give Brendan an extra second to get the ball downfield."

For a split second, everyone on the field froze, eyes wide and mouths hanging open. Then Don pulled on his helmet, clapped his hands together, pulled Thomas aside, and called out, "Let's go! Blitz from the left. I'll show you."

After exchanging a few stunned glances, the makeshift lines got set, the ball was snapped, and sure enough, Don squared up to take the rusher head-on. With the extra time, Brendan sent a perfect spiral downfield to Wickie.

"You got it?" Don asked. Thomas nodded. "Okay, get in there," he said, maneuvering Thomas back into place. "And remember—square your hips."

They ran the same play again, and this time Thomas stood the oncoming rusher straight up, once again giving Brendan enough time to hit Wickie in stride twenty yards out.

"Well, what do you think about that?" I turned to face Austin, but he'd already hopped up and was jogging toward the center of the field, where he gave both Brendan and Thomas hearty pats on the back.

"Tony!" Owen's voice boomed from several yards down the sideline.

As the guys lined up to run another play, I made my way to meet him. He was positively beaming.

"I see Don is out on the field. I take it Joe's had a change of heart."

"No, I'm afraid not." Owen's face fell. "But it looks like Don might have," I said.

"Well, what about Sunday?" Owen asked with concern. "Any chance he gets into the game?"

"That's not my call, but I'd be surprised," I hedged. "Joe's tenacity seems to have paid off, though. I think these guys may have finally turned the corner."

"What does that mean?" Owen asked.

"It means that what's happening out there—" I pointed to the cluster of offensive and defensive players . . . stars, rookies, and backups—"is something I don't think this franchise has ever experienced before. Owen, I'd guess this is the first time these guys have truly played as a *team* since you started the Vipers." Owen turned and watched as Brendan hit Wesley midstride at the 10 yard line.

"Trust me, Owen," I said, clapping him on the back. "What you're seeing here is exactly what you want to see."

Owen just sighed and shook his head. "What I'd really like to see is Don back in the starting lineup. I hope you boys know what you're doing. Perry's been surveying the landscape, and we're *still* not a lock to pass that referendum. We have *got* to win this week!"

•　　•　　•　　•　　•

We didn't.

Brendan played well in spite of being rushed all night, though he did suffer a pick-six when a hurried pass was tipped at the line. For his part, Thomas did a fantastic job standing up against the Bucs pass rush, but in the end, Tampa's aerial assault proved too much for the Vipers secondary, and we lost 21–10.

As expected, the atmosphere in the locker room following the game was bleak. When I got there, Brendan was still sitting in front of his locker holding his helmet between his knees and staring at the floor. Even though he'd played well, I'm sure he blamed himself for the loss. He was quickly joined by Austin, who did his best to console him.

On the opposite side of the room, Don was congratulating Thomas. The backup had run for forty-five yards, and though he did get called for a hold late in the third, Brendan had escaped the game sack-free. When Don saw Austin encouraging Brendan, however, his smile quickly faded. Giving Thomas one last congratulatory pat on the shoulder, he slowly made his way across the room toward Austin and Brendan. As Austin stood up, Don knelt in front of Brendan. Though Don's back was to me, I assumed by the way Brendan was shaking his head that Don was telling him he'd played a solid game. Then Don stood and faced Austin, and the two spoke.

Fun fact: If you spend enough time in the broadcasting booth, you get to be pretty good at lipreading. There was far too much commotion to make out what was actually said, but I'm pretty sure I saw Don say "I'm sorry" and "I promise—it will never happen again."

Austin's softening expression confirmed my suspicion. Then he reached out and shook Don's hand.

When I looked up, I noticed Joe standing in the doorway, and one glimpse told me he'd seen exactly what I had. As Don grabbed his jacket out of his locker, Joe came up behind him. Not wanting to miss this exchange, I worked my way across the room, stopping a few feet away but within earshot.

"Don?"

He snapped to attention. "Yes, Coach?"

"I heard about what you did after practice the other day."

"I was just trying to help," he said, struggling to make eye contact.

"Well . . . ," Joe started, seemingly thrown by the confident veteran's uncharacteristically humble demeanor, "you enjoy your bye week."

"Yes, sir."

I realized I had been holding my breath, waiting for Don to ask Joe if he'd be playing against Philly in two weeks. But then Joe turned and started to walk away, leaving the veteran to finish packing up his bag.

"Oh, and Don?" Joe said, looking back over his shoulder, "I expect to see you here bright and early a week from Monday." His mouth curled into a smile. "We need to get ready for Philly."

PART IV

The Payoff

SIGHT ADJUSTMENT

THE LOSS TO TAMPA ASIDE, the Vipers' bye week could not have come at a better time. It not only gave Austin and a host of other dinged-up players an extra week to recover but also coincided with the annual Citrus State Showdown. At Perry's suggestion, Owen hosted both schools' presidents in his private box. After the game, Owen treated a handful of trustees from the two schools to a tour of the facilities, culminating in a stop in his office, where he gave them a sneak peek at the architect's rendering of the new stadium.

According to Terry, the afternoon had made quite an impact on Owen.

"I wish you could have been there," Terry laughed, his voice filling my home office via speakerphone. "Those guys couldn't have handled Owen better if we had coached them!"

"Did you?" I asked.

"Not one bit," Terry insisted. "Honestly, I think Perry just figured it would be a nice goodwill gesture—letting them sit in Owen's box, giving them a personal tour—but if you could have seen the look on Owen's face when they told him how much of an impact the revenue from that game had on their respective scholarship funds and what a devastating blow it would be to lose that . . . Tony, it was priceless."

"Terry, that's awesome!"

"That's not even the best part," he continued. "When Owen was showing the trustees the artist's drawings of the new stadium, one of them interrupted him mid–sales pitch and asked him how much ticket prices were going to be."

"Uh-oh," I chuckled.

"Tony, when Owen told that poor woman roughly what it would run a family of four to attend a game, her chin almost hit the floor. Of course, Owen had probably spent more than that on the suit he was wearing, so it took him a few seconds to realize that the mood of the room had shifted. I think what really got to him, though, was when the woman looked out his window at the field and said, 'But I'm guessing you'll have a pretty good view.'"

I laughed out loud. "No, she didn't."

"Yes, she did!" Terry laughed back.

"Wow. I would love to have seen that."

Terry's call was practically an answer to prayer. As exciting as it had been to watch the coaches and players begin to rally around the SOUL principles, I'd been racking my brain trying to figure out a way to get Owen to understand the importance of his role and the impact his proposal would have on the community. From the looks of it, though, the Showdown might have just done it for me.

"Was that Terry's voice I heard?" Lauren asked, popping her head around my door.

I nodded, a smile still etched on my face.

"What were you two laughing about?" She eyed me suspiciously.

I got up from behind my desk, walked over, and hugged her. "The price of an Armani suit," I joked.

"What?"

I'd tell her the full story later. For now, I just wanted to savor the moment.

●　　●　　●　　●　　●

The one downside of the bye week was that it gave the media extra time to heap criticism on the team's record following the loss to the Bucs. According to the *Press*, the Vipers were officially "a team in crisis." After all, the Falcons now led the division at 8–3, and the Bucs and Eagles were 7–4—two games ahead of the Vipers in the wild card race. The local columnists also had plenty to say about Joe's decision to sit the team's perfectly healthy All-Pro running back for two straight weeks. Fortunately, at Gym's urging, Joe was avoiding picking up the sports page as much as possible these days and doing his best to stay focused on the positive strides the team was making.

And the Vipers *had* made a lot of improvements. They'd managed to beat the Packers with two of their best players not even dressing for the game, Whit and DC were getting along better than anyone on staff could remember, and even Wickie had become a force for good. He was playing well week in and week out, doing whatever the game plan called for without complaint, and of late, even taking a special interest in Wesley's development.

Following the bye, with both Austin and Don back in, the team faced Philly at home. I was there for the game. The Vipers as a whole played well, and though they weren't able to move the ball on the ground very effectively, Don, who was limited to only sixteen yards rushing, proved to be an effective blocker, giving Austin time to connect on multiple passing plays.

With just under four minutes remaining in the fourth quarter, the Vipers trailed 17–14. We were facing second and eight from our own 27 yard line, roughly forty-five yards out of field goal range.

The Eagles had been playing a soft zone off the line against our receivers all game. Austin had been picking it apart, so Whit called for a Double Left, Scat Right, 844 H-wheel.

Wesley was in the slot out to the left and would be running a hook pattern back to Austin just short of the down marker. The tight end would head about ten yards downfield, then run a dig: turn ninety degrees and run parallel to the line of scrimmage in the middle of the field, with Wickie running an out pattern and breaking toward the sideline, also at about ten yards out.

Since they needed eight yards for a first down, the hope was that either the dig or the out would be open near the first down marker. Wesley's route, which was a yard or two shy of the marker, was basically a safety valve for Austin in case the others weren't open.

When they lined up, however, the Eagles showed man coverage on the receivers for the first time all day.

They're going to double cover Wickie, I realized.

It made sense. After all, he was among the league leaders in receptions and already had nine catches on the day. Wesley, on the other hand, had struggled to get off the line cleanly and, as a result, hadn't been targeted that afternoon.

Given the coverage, the receivers were coached to spot the situation and adjust their route accordingly. The tight end and Wickie would stick with their routes as called, but Wesley had the responsibility to sight adjust and switch his hook to a go route against bump-and-run coverage—to sprint straight down the field—provided, of course, that he could get off the line clean without being pushed off his route by the cornerback.

Come on, Wesley. See the coverage. Get off that line.

As soon as the ball was snapped, Wesley executed a perfect swim move, got his pads under and around the cornerback, and took off straight down the field.

Austin dropped back, glanced right to hold the safeties, then turned his shoulders and released the pass deep, down the left hash marks. Every eye in the coaches booth was glued to Wesley, so none of us even saw Don's block on the blitzing linebacker until the replay.

We all instinctively rose to our feet as Austin's pass sailed downfield, hitting Wesley—in stride—at the 30 yard line, where this rookie from the Eagles of Carson-Newman University left the Eagles of the National Football League in his wake as he raced the final distance for the touchdown.

The coaches booth erupted in celebratory cheers and high fives as Wesley was tackled from behind five yards deep in the end zone. No penalty flag was thrown, however, since the aggressor wasn't an Eagle but rather Wickie Ariet, who had been sprinting downfield along with nine other Vipers who were blocking for the rookie.

"I knew we were right to keep that kid!" Whit shouted. Then he caught Stan's eye and self-corrected. "That is, I knew *you* were right to keep that kid."

The two exchanged pats on the back and then settled back into their seats. Patrick Kingsby nailed the extra point, putting us up 21–17 with just under three minutes remaining.

That's when everything almost fell apart. A Vipers defender slipped on the turf on the ensuing kickoff, allowing the Eagles returner to take the ball all the way down to the Vipers' 2 yard line, where he was finally pushed out-of-bounds.

The coaches booth went from sheer euphoria to complete devastation in just under thirty seconds.

It's all riding on the defense now.

Whit leaned forward in his seat, his fingers steepled against his lips, while three seats down, DC went into full-on run-stop mode.

On the first down, Louis Blackstock shot through a gap and tackled the Eagles running back for a two-yard loss. Whit exhaled so loudly that even DC heard it and turned to give Whit a reassuring fist pump. On the next play, the running back powered through and was tackled at the 1 yard line. It was third and goal with 2:12 left, the clock running. Whit took his hat off and ran a visibly shaky hand through his hair.

"Hold 'em, guys," said Stan, rocking back and forth in his seat, eyes fixed on the goal line.

Down on the Vipers sideline, the entire roster was standing and watching, which was unusual given there was still time left on the clock. Normally the offense would all be sitting on the bench, consulting with one another and their tablets, adjusting their gear, and getting ready for their next series. But every last player was locked in on what was happening down inside the 5 yard line, as were all the coaches—offensive, defensive, and special teams alike.

I can't remember the last time I've seen that.

With the play clock down to :01, the Eagles snapped the ball. The quarterback dropped back, turned to his left, and threw a soft-arcing pass toward the back post, sailing just inches over the receiver's head and sending the crowd, the Vipers sideline, and the coaches booth into delirium.

Down by four and still on the 1, the Eagles decided to go for it on fourth down.

As the defense got into position, the Vipers offense turned away from the field and motioned with their arms for the crowd to raise the volume—a redundant gesture since the raucous crowd was already emitting a deafening roar.

"Come on," Whit called out intently, both hands curled into fists. "Stuff the run!" When the defense did just that, tackling the running back behind the line of scrimmage, the entire stadium erupted, and DC found himself on the receiving end of a congratulatory bear hug from the last person he'd have expected.

"All right, it's all yours," DC said, pushing Whit back and smiling. "Now let's finish this thing and get out of here."

Whit took a deep breath, returned to his seat, and repositioned his headset.

"Get the line together," he ordered his assistant down on the sideline. "Tell them there are—" he glanced over at the scoreboard—"two minutes, four seconds left in this game." Carefully emphasizing each word, he added, *And we are not giving the ball back.*

One of the offensive coaches called up to Whit. "Look at Wickie. He's only got one man near him. The safeties are all up to play the run. We could . . ."

"No," Whit cut him off. "We're running the ball to get a first down, then kneeling on it. Nothing cute. No passes. Let's just get the win and get out of here," he said, shooting a quick wink over to DC.

Whit paused for a second, then checked to make sure his instructions were heard loud and clear against the still-screaming crowd. "Do you hear me? Hand the ball off to Don. Make sure he stays in bounds. The Eagles are out of time-outs, so all we need is one first down, and this game is ours." He turned and nodded at DC. "Let's run out the clock."

Starting from our own 3 yard line, the Vipers did just that. Don's first run brought them out to the 7, giving the offense a little breathing room heading into the two-minute warning.

The next play saw Don tackled for no gain, but the clock continued to run. With the clock ticking down to 1:36, Austin handed the ball off to Don again, who fought his way up to the 12 yard line. First down.

The crowd erupted as the offense took a knee. Game over.

Afterward, Wesley told anyone who would listen that Wickie had taken him aside right before his big catch and reminded him about his sight adjustments if he got bump coverage from the Eagles. To his credit, Wickie brushed the comments aside and instead credited the rookie with making a great catch.

That game ended up being the first of three straight wins, quieting the calls for Joe's job. Coupled with an unexpected Tampa loss to Buffalo, the Vipers were suddenly tied for the final playoff spot with two games left to play, both on the road—one at Tennessee and the season finale at Tampa.

Seeing Is Believing

We came close in Tennessee, fighting back from a twelve-point deficit in the fourth, only to lose on a controversial incomplete end zone pass from Austin to Wickie in the final seconds of the game.

"Dad," Justin had complained after the game, "we have *got* to figure out what counts as a catch in this league!"

Even I thought Wickie had "survived the ground" on that play, but there simply wasn't a replay angle clear enough to support it and overturn the call on the field.

"Those are the rules, Justin," I said with a shrug. "You can't control everything. All you can do is play your best."

In the meantime, the Bucs won their game, regaining the lead in the wild card race. A win over the Buccaneers would pull us even, and since each team would have beaten the other once, tiebreakers such as division and conference records would come into play—and those fell in our favor. In short, the winner of this game would be the only team on Interstate 4 to make the playoffs this season.

Being in Tampa, this matchup was technically a home game for me, even though I sat with Owen and Terry in the visiting owners box. Despite a feverish crowd and an early deficit when the Bucs ran the opening kickoff back for a touchdown, the Vipers hung in there. Don broke a long run for a touchdown to tie the score in the first before the Bucs took the lead again with a field goal. Then in the second, Austin found Wickie in the end zone to put us up 14–10. Just before the half, Louis picked off a pass on an out route and ran it back for a touchdown.

21–10, Vipers.

"It's like looking at a different team," Terry said, shaking his head in amazement.

"They *are* playing well," Owen agreed. "Another thirty minutes like that, and we'll be playoff bound!"

And that's exactly what happened. Wickie caught his second touchdown pass of the day, and the defense continued to shut down Tampa's offense. By the middle of the fourth quarter, Joe was comfortable enough with his lead to pull Austin, Wickie, Don, and a handful of other starters, to avoid their getting hurt on a meaningless play.

"Unbelievable," Terry exclaimed as the final seconds ran off the clock. Then he turned to me, shaking his head in disbelief, and said, "You did it, Tony."

I immediately put up my palms to deflect the comment. "Hey, I didn't do anything. They did." I pointed toward the field where the two teams mingled after the game, a number of players from both teams kneeling in prayer in the middle of the field.

Owen looked back and forth between me and Terry, then pointed down at the field. "You mean to tell me that all of this is due to those SOUL things you talked about?"

Terry smiled and looked directly at his boss. "They are a different *team*, Owen."

Owen stared down at the field for a few more seconds before looking back at me quizzically. "Wickie's always been a great receiver. He hasn't changed."

"Oh, I beg to differ," I said. "He's changed . . . a lot."

Owen just shrugged it off. "Well, I don't see it."

"Come on," Terry said, reluctantly accepting defeat. "Let's head down to the locker room and congratulate Joe."

Owen was still staring absently at the field. "I just don't see it," he muttered, then grabbed his jacket and followed Terry out of the box.

●　　●　　●　　●　　●

To say that the mood in the visitors' locker room was jubilant would have been an understatement. As I glanced toward the ceiling, I was surprised to see that someone had hung banners that read "Win for each other! Win for the fans! Win to inspire!" and "Play with SOUL out there today!" They were almost exact duplicates of the ones that had been hanging in the Vipers' locker room all season.

"Nice, aren't they?" Gym sidled up beside me, all smiles. "Mark had them printed up for us. We've had them at every away game this season."

Well, how about that.

After a few more minutes of revelry, Joe made his way to the center of the room and waved the group quiet with his arms. He had a football in each hand.

After congratulating the entire team on a hard-fought, well-played game, he awarded a game ball to the entire Vipers defense for completely shutting down the number one passing offense in the league.

DC accepted on their behalf, with Whit leading the cheers.

Then Joe quieted the room once again.

"The other game ball goes to Wickie Ariet!"

Wickie stepped forward as the chant "Wick, Wick, Wick" filled the room.

Joe handed him the ball. "Fantastic game, Wickie. Six catches, two for touchdowns, which brings your total catches for the season to—"

He turned to Gym for help.

"Ninety-nine," Gym said, checking his stat sheet.

Once again, the room erupted in cheers and applause as a wildly grinning Owen made his way to the center of the room to shake Wickie's hand.

I was all caught up in the celebration myself when I noticed Joe's expression had changed dramatically.

"All right, guys, let's shower up," Joe called out, a forced smile on his face. "Great game, everyone."

As the team scattered to take their showers and get ready to board the bus back to Orlando, I watched Joe hold Wickie back.

"Something wrong, Coach?" the still-grinning wide receiver asked.

"Why didn't you say something?" Joe asked as Owen, Gym, Whit, and I looked on.

"About what?" Wickie seemed genuinely confused.

Joe held up the stat sheet. "Ninety-nine."

Wickie smiled slightly, then bowed his head.

"I don't get it," Owen broke in. "What's ninety-nine?"

"Ninety-nine catches!" Whit said, his palm slapping his forehead as he realized what Joe was getting at.

"You only needed *one more*," Joe said.

"I know," Wickie replied, his voice confident.

"You *knew*?" Gym asked.

Wickie turned and flashed us all a sly smile. "This may surprise some of you, but I do keep track of my stats."

"What's he talking about?" Owen asked.

"Wickie's contract calls for a $250,000 bonus if he finishes the regular season with one hundred catches," Gym responded.

Owen turned a stunned glance back toward Wickie.

"I had no . . . no *idea* that's where you were," Joe stammered. "You should've said something. I wouldn't have pulled you! We were up by 17 and could have easily gotten one more pass to you . . ."

Poor Joe—the guy looked positively gutted. I knew that feeling well. The same thing happened to me in Indy with Reggie Wayne. Like Joe, I sat Reggie to avoid injury heading into the playoffs, completely unaware that he was only three catches away from a hefty bonus. Like Wickie, he never said a word. Still, until now, I would never have compared the two—at least not in terms of character. Reggie was selfless to a fault. Wickie was not, but now he was at least . . . *different* somehow.

Wickie shrugged. "Hey," he replied, "we won, right? That's what matters." And with that, the wide receiver winked at Joe, flashed the rest of us a wide grin, and headed back toward his locker.

Gym, Joe, Terry, and I all stared at one another, stunned.

Finally, Owen broke the silence. "Okay," he said, turning to face Terry and me. "Now I think I see it."

BETTER LATE
THAN NEVER

HEADING INTO JANUARY, the good news definitely outweighed the bad. The Vipers were in the playoffs for the first time in franchise history, and apart from the usual late-season dings and dents, the entire roster was healthy.

As the fifth seed, however, they would not have a home play-off game—a downside that disappointed everyone, especially Owen. Despite Mark's brilliant season-long marketing campaign, near-constant press coverage thanks to Perry, and a spot in the playoffs, the latest in-house polls still showed mixed community support for the upcoming referendum vote, and Owen had been hoping a home playoff game would help push the city over the top.

Instead, it was off to Dallas for round one.

Interestingly, Dallas had looked to be out of the race until they signed the ever-controversial Fred Ashford midseason after Miami let him go. Fred put up a great string of games for them, clinching the Cowboys a spot in the playoffs. Given Ashford's dominance, Joe's game plan hinged on keeping the Cowboys offense off the field as much as possible. Because it was the playoffs, I accompanied the team on this road game, once again sitting with Owen and Terry in the visiting owners box. As expected, the Cowboys fans had packed the stadium, though I spotted several small pockets of green and black mixed in among the sea of silver, navy, and white.

Whit and DC were both at the top of their games, with the Vipers offense chewing up yardage and owning time of possession, and the defense doing their part to keep Ashford and the rest of the Cowboys offense out of the end zone.

The Vipers led 7–6 at the half, and thanks to the suddenly on-fire Patrick Kingsby's three successive fifty-plus-yard field goals, we were still up—16–12—late in the fourth quarter.

Austin was in shotgun formation when the normally flawless Vipers center sent the snap sailing almost a foot over Austin's head. A melee ensued and the Vipers eventually recovered the ball, but not before an attainable third and five from the Cowboys forty-five became fourth and forever from our own thirty-eight. We were forced to punt, giving Fred Ashford one last chance to beat the team that had passed on signing him twice that season.

"I swear, if we end up losing this game because of *that* guy . . . ," Owen exclaimed, gesturing toward Ashford as the lanky receiver took the field.

"O ye of little faith," replied Terry, smiling.

As everyone expected, Dallas looked to their star, calling three straight passing plays, all targeting Ashford. What nobody expected was for Vipers backup corner Cornelius Brooks, who came in late in the third after the starter rolled his ankle, to stay with the future Hall of Famer step for step and effectively swat away all three passes.

One punt, a short return, three straight running plays called by Whit, and a kneel down later, we were headed to the divisional-round playoff game in San Francisco.

Terry was all smiles. "Come on, Owen. Let's head down to the locker room."

"In a minute," Owen said, grabbing his jacket. "I want to go down and see this place from the field."

I didn't blame him. The Cowboys stadium *was* a sight to behold. With a sticker price of $1.2 billion, it was right up there with the new Falcons stadium in Atlanta—roughly $300 million less than the projected cost for the proposed Vipers stadium.

We followed Owen onto the field, where he walked right to the giant star on the 50 yard line. We gazed up at the massive 11,500-square-foot video screen above.

"Man," he uttered, craning his head back. "Will you look at that?"

It *was* impressive. Cornelius Brooks had even run back out onto the field in his T-shirt to take a picture of the final score up on the screen.

After gazing up and around the stadium for another minute or two, Owen checked his watch and said, "All right, gentlemen, I do believe there's a party waiting!" But before we reached the sideline, a flash of lime green off to the left caught our attention. There in the end zone was Wickie, signing autographs for a group of young kids all decked out in Vipers gear.

"Well, now I've seen everything," said Terry.

"O ye of little faith," I echoed back at him.

Suddenly, one of the kids pointed behind Wickie and started jumping up and down excitedly, causing the wide receiver to whip his head around. A sly smile crept across his face.

"Hey, Brooksie!" he called out to the startled backup. "Get on over here and give these kids your autograph!"

As Cornelius headed over to the kids and started signing what appeared to be Quarles and Ariet jerseys, Terry turned to me. "Well, what do you think about that?"

"Do we even carry a Brooks jersey?" Owen asked.

"Nope," said Terry, smiling and nodding toward the kids. "They don't care. Those are Robinson's Road Warriors. They're just excited to meet a real, live player face-to-face."

"They're who?" Owen asked.

"Robinson's Road Warriors," Terry repeated. "The last few weeks, Wesley Robinson has been renting a luxury box at road games for a group of at-risk kids from the downtown Orlando Boys Club—flies them out to the game and everything. That's their chaperone over there," he said, pointing to a man sitting about five rows back and wearing the same black T-shirt the kids were wearing. "Robinson's Road Warriors" was written in lime green across the front.

"That's got to cost a pretty penny," Owen mused. I could tell he was calculating the cost of box seats, airfare, hotels, and meals for ten kids and an adult against a sixth-round rookie's salary.

Terry just shrugged and smiled. "The kid wants to give something back. You know, his version of the *L* in SOUL—of making the community better." Then he slapped Owen on the shoulder. "Come on, Owen," he said. "You've got some celebrating to do!"

Owen turned and followed Terry back to the locker room, but for some reason, he looked more thoughtful than celebratory.

Win-Win

LATER THAT NIGHT, as we were headed back to Orlando, I got up and moved into the seat next to the pensive owner.

"You okay, Owen?" I asked. "I thought you'd be a lot happier about all of this."

He just stared out the window into the darkness. When he spoke, he sounded exhausted. "I've been thinking . . . that stadium back there—" he absently gestured over his shoulder in the general direction of Dallas—"it's beautiful. But what Robinson's doing for those kids? That's . . . that's something else."

"Beautiful too. It's definitely very generous of him," I agreed.

"That's just it," Owen continued. "I mean . . . you've got Wickie shrugging off a quarter-of-a-million-dollar bonus like it was nothing, and everyone put in loads of extra time helping Brendan get up to speed when Austin got hurt. Joe even put his job on the line by refusing to play Don." He laughed. "I just feel like I'm the only one around here who hasn't done anything for anybody—the only one who hasn't sacrificed anything to get here." He looked down at the floor.

I let Owen wrestle for a few minutes with what he'd said.

Finally, I looked over at him. "You know, there's a verse in the New Testament that I've always loved and tried to live my life by," I remarked. Owen turned his head and looked back at me. "It's something my mother used to tell me all the time when I was growing up: 'What do you benefit if you gain the whole world but lose your own soul?'"

Owen held my gaze intently for a few seconds and then sat back. Sighing deeply, he stared back out the window in silence.

●　　●　　●　　●　　●

As we flew into Orlando, we noticed that the entire city was awash in lime green. The lights in the SunTrust Center were even lit up to read "We ♥ Our Vipers."

"Gentlemen," Owen said, breaking the silence, "I know it's late, but I'm wondering if you wouldn't mind meeting in my office after we land."

The three of us exchanged confused glances, and a chorus of "Sure, Owen" quickly followed.

Owen turned to Terry. "Terry, can you please call Mark King and Perry Richards and ask them to meet us there? I'm sure they'll still be up."

Terry nodded and reached into his breast pocket for his phone.

"And believe me," Owen said with a smile as we began our final approach, "they'll both want to hear this."

●　　●　　●　　●　　●

By the time we landed and made our way over to the stadium, Mark and Perry were already waiting for us outside Owen's office.

"What's going on?" a bleary-eyed Mark asked me after Owen strode past us and opened the door.

I just shrugged and said, "Your guess is as good as mine. By the way, how are Ashley and the new baby doing?"

"They're doing great, Tony. Thanks for asking."

"Everybody have a seat," Owen said, riffling through the stacks of papers on his desk. I took a step toward one of the giant leather chairs, then thought better of it and took a seat next to Gym on the sectional.

As poor Perry unexpectedly sank into one of the chairs, drawing a chuckle from Mark, a rejuvenated Owen handed a file to Terry.

"I want to redefine the terms of the stadium deal," Owen announced matter-of-factly.

"What?" Terry asked, his confused expression mirroring the rest of ours.

"We need to fix this thing . . . get it right," Owen continued, now pacing back and forth in front of his desk.

Terry looked down at the extensive file in his hands, then stared blankly at Owen. "But the city council has approved these terms," he said. "It's already on the ballot. You can't change it now."

"Oh, they'll change it," Owen said emphatically. "I guarantee it!"

While Terry searched for his next question, I offered up one of my own.

"Change it how, exactly?"

"The way I see it," Owen said, growing more and more animated, "there are two basic issues that need to be fixed. First, we need to pay a bigger share of the construction costs, and second, we need to rethink the revenue split."

Terry stared at Owen, speechless.

"You want to *what*?" Gym asked.

"Right now, we're only paying one-eighth of the total cost, and technically, we're not even paying that; we're borrowing it from the league," he explained. "Here's what I'm proposing . . ."

He paused briefly while Terry fished a pen out of his breast pocket and flipped over the folder to write on the back. When he looked back up, Owen began.

"If the league will pay an eighth, the city an eighth, and the state an eighth," he said, pausing to let Terry catch up, "I'll take care of the rest."

Terry stared at him. The pen didn't move.

"What?" Terry finally asked.

The rest of us were stunned as well.

"That's . . . a pretty hefty chunk of change, Owen," Gym said, understating the impact of Owen's proposal.

"It is. And why not?" Owen shot back. "I can afford it. Besides, we'll make it back in advertising in no time. Right, Mark?" He gestured toward the dumbstruck marketing director.

"Why . . . uh . . . yeah!" Mark stammered, a smile spreading across his face.

"And of course, we'll get the revenue from all our home games and naming rights," Owen quickly continued.

"But," he paused, "I want to split the revenues straight down the middle from all the other events hosted at the stadium—fifty-fifty, the city and the Vipers—until we earn back the full construction costs. Then we'll go to thirty-seventy— they get the seventy. Except," he paused again, "for the Citrus State Showdown. I want to grandfather that in," he said directly to Terry. "The schools keep *all* revenues from that event in per-petuity. And no matter where it falls on our schedule," he added emphatically, "that event stays right here in Orlando."

"Speaking of which," Perry hesitantly asked, "am I correct in assuming that moving to Oakland is officially off the table?"

"Oh, it's off the table, my friend," Owen answered, beaming. "This team belongs to the city of Orlando, and we'll stay here as long as they'll have us."

The room fell silent for a moment while Gym, Terry, Mark, Perry, and I all exchanged bewildered looks that turned into smiles.

Finally, I spoke for the group. "Owen, this is—" I searched for the right word—"*overwhelming.*" Then to make sure this wasn't a whim, I asked, "Are you sure you want to do this?"

Owen smiled. In a calm and measured voice, he said, "Tony, I've never been more sure of anything in my life."

"Well, that's all I need to hear," said Terry, rising to his feet. "Owen, I'll have these terms typed up and see if I can get an appointment with the city council tomorrow afternoon— Tuesday at the latest." The normally stoic judge was grinning from ear to ear.

"And Owen," he said, holding out his hand, "thank you."

Owen took his good friend's hand in his, looked him in the eye, and said, "No, thank you." Then, looking at each of us individually, he remarked, "Thanks to *all* of you."

As the five of us left Owen's office, I turned to a still-speechless Gym, smiled, and commented, "I told you he'd get it."

"O *we* of little faith," said Terry.

CHAMPIONSHIP
SHOWDOWN

LAUREN WAS SO BLOWN AWAY by Owen's change of heart that she didn't even mind my getting home so late that night.

"Tony," she said, shaking her head in disbelief, "what you just described is nothing short of a miracle."

It wouldn't be the last one either. The next day, Owen and Terry met with the city council to present the new deal points. After the stunned council members regained the power of speech, they enthusiastically agreed to change the ballot. Later that night, Terry called and told me that Owen had also decided to freeze ticket prices for the next three seasons and to reserve one luxury box at each home game for a local charitable organization, rotating with each game.

All week, the local papers extolled the miraculous by dividing their ink equally between the playoff win and upcoming game and Owen's change of heart on the stadium deal.

The miracles continued the following Sunday when the Vipers upset the top-seeded 49ers 30–13 to stamp their ticket to the NFC championship game. Even those of us who thought the Vipers had a chance of pulling off the upset were surprised by the margin of victory. It ended up being one of those games where the higher seed couldn't get out of its own way after a week off with a bye. Fumbles, interceptions, and penalties plagued San Francisco all day, and the outcome was never in doubt.

By the time the team returned to Orlando early Monday morning, the entire city had caught Viper fever.

•　　•　　•　　•　　•

I arrived at the stadium on Wednesday just in time to hear the fireworks. Someone was screaming bloody murder in the offensive meeting room, and for once, it wasn't Whit.

Moments later, a furious Don Buerkle stormed out past me before disappearing around the corner. I turned back to the meeting room to see an exhausted-looking Joe standing in the doorway.

"What happened?" I asked. Joe sighed and waved me into the room, where Whit and Gym were leaning on the conference table, their faces lined with concern.

"Tony," Joe began, "we've decided to throw the ball this week—almost exclusively."

Even though Joe's opening comments needed no further explanation, he continued to put their logic into words for me. "The Falcons beat us twice this season, both times pretty badly. Their defense completely shut down the run. I don't think Don had twenty yards between both games."

I remembered those two games well. There was no question about it—the Falcons definitely keyed in on Don during both.

"So," Whit picked up where Joe had left off, "we have two choices: Either stick with a balanced offense, knowing it will be tough to run, and hope our D can make it a low-scoring game . . ."

"Or," Joe jumped back in, "be aggressive and come out

throwing, knowing that they're going to crowd the line of scrimmage against the run."

I thought about their options. "Well, if I'm remembering correctly, you tried the first approach twice, and both games got totally out of hand."

"That they did," Gym sighed, tapping his fingers on the table.

I nodded at Gym, then looked back at Whit and Joe. "Austin's been throwing the ball well all year, and between Wickie and Wesley, you've got both sides of the field covered. I think you need to stay true to your convictions, and the passing game is definitely a strength. There's no point in trying to run the ball against a team that's completely shut you down twice already."

"That's what we were thinking," said Gym.

"The problem is, in order to protect Austin against the blitz once they realize we're abandoning the run," Joe continued, "we're going to need Don out there—"

"Blocking," I finished.

"Almost exclusively," added Gym.

"So what I heard earlier was—"

"Don having a difference of opinion with our game plan," said Joe.

It has never ceased to amaze me how elation can change to devastation at the drop of a hat in this league.

"So . . . ," I said, looking at Joe, "what's your plan?"

"Well, we suspended him before," Gym said reluctantly.

Whit looked like he was going to be sick, and I didn't blame him. Sure, the team had played well in Don's absence against the Packers, but benching him in the biggest game, not only of the season but also in franchise history, seemed unthinkable— even to me. And besides, if the Vipers really wanted to throw, they needed Don out there so the Falcons would focus on stopping him.

I decided to throw out a third option.

"Joe, why don't you let me talk to him? You're all too close to this right now. Emotions are running high. You don't want to say something you might regret."

Joe looked over at Whit, then Gym. Both nodded in agreement.

"Okay," he conceded, "see what you can do."

After checking the locker room, the weight room, and the training room, I finally found Don sitting in the stadium, three rows up from the field level. His forearms were resting on his knees, and his blank stare was directed at the snake head painted on the middle of the field. It had faded in the weeks since the Vipers had played their final home game, but the barely visible fangs seemed an appropriate backdrop for the moment.

"Hey, Don," I said, climbing up the stands and taking a seat next to him.

"Coach," he said, his eyes not leaving the field. "Sorry I almost ran into you back there."

"That's okay," I laughed. "I used to be a defensive back, you know. We're a pretty tough group."

That got a chuckle out of him. I decided to take advantage of the slight crack in his facade.

"You do know that even if you don't carry the ball, you're still important to what they're doing here, don't you?"

"Yeah," Don said. Then he turned to face me, and with emotion filling his voice, he nearly shouted, "But this is the most important game in franchise history, and I'm not even gonna get the ball!"

"No, probably not," I agreed, keeping my voice calm and level. "At least not much. But that doesn't mean you won't be helping the team—that they don't need you."

"Sure," he scoffed. "As a decoy and a blocker." His voice was tinged with sarcasm.

"Exactly," I said, catching him off guard. "You might not think it's important, but blocking, being a distraction, drawing the defense's attention away from the receivers, and protecting Austin, those are all critical pieces of this game plan. They still need you every bit as much as they always have," I argued. "Your role just looks a little different—*this week*." He looked out across the field and squinted at the sun.

"But it *is* your role, Don," I continued. "And you know that, right?"

He pursed his lips and looked down at the ground, then over at me. "And if I don't?"

I knew he was expecting me to tell him that Coach Webster would scratch him from the game. But if there's one thing I've learned in all my years of coaching, it's that often the best option is the one no one is expecting.

"Then everyone loses."

Sold Out

Usually when a team throws more than fifty passes in a game, it means they're far behind, desperate to catch up . . . but not in this case. The sold-out crowd in Atlanta had been treated to a masterfully called offensive game by Whit. Don carried the ball only twice in the first three quarters, just as he'd feared. And each time, the Falcons defense dropped him for a loss. With the run game shut down, Whit spread Austin's passes out among a variety of receivers and tight ends, keeping the defense off-balance.

On the other side of the ball, DC's unit played almost flaw-lessly. Atlanta struggled more on offense than they had in the two regular season meetings, and in the fourth quarter, the Falcons were clinging to a 24–22 lead. They were driving, how-ever, and taking precious time off the clock.

I sat with Owen and Terry once again, our collective blood pressure rising as we watched the Falcons continue to push the Vipers back toward the goal line.

The two-minute warning came and went, and when play

resumed, the Falcons were facing a third and goal from the 4. A field goal would mean we would need to score a touchdown to win, while a touchdown would put them up by nine points, all but clinching their berth in the Super Bowl.

We all sat breathless as Louis Blackstock shot through a gap in the Falcons offensive line, hitting the running back just as he took the handoff, popping the ball out of his hands. Cornelius Brooks caught it in midair and began streaking toward the end zone, over ninety yards away.

Owen, Terry, and I sprang from our seats, along with roughly seventy thousand panicking Falcons fans and a smattering of Vipers fans wearing lime green up in the nosebleed seats. Almost as soon as the excitement started, it ended, as Cornelius was tripped up by the diving Falcons quarterback at our 15 yard line, leaving us with eighty-five yards to go and only a minute and thirty seconds left.

An incomplete pass by Austin, just off Wesley's fingertips, brought up second down. Second down was almost a complete disaster, as the Falcons pass rush completely overwhelmed the offensive line, and Austin was barely able to heave the ball out-of-bounds before he was sacked, bringing up third and ten—still on our own 15. One minute and eighteen seconds remained.

The noise from the crowd was deafening.

As substitutions took place, Don reentered the game, as did Thomas, the backup running back, who lined up to the right. It was a pick-your-poison option from Whit, and he had chosen to protect Austin. We would have fewer receivers to run routes, but extra blockers to give Austin enough time to pass.

The play looked to be another debacle from the outset. The Falcons timed the snap perfectly, and it was a jailbreak, with two Falcons defenders coming unblocked from the left. It looked for all the world as if Austin would have no shot to get a pass off, either to Wickie coming across the middle on a dig route, or to Wesley, running a post on the other side.

Suddenly, out of nowhere, Don flashed in front of Austin, somehow launching himself sideways in front of both oncoming rushers. He hit them with such velocity that he was actually flung backward at Austin's feet, but his sacrifice gave the quarterback just enough time to get the ball out to Wickie.

Wickie caught the perfectly placed ball in stride, then streaked across the middle and turned up the field. He was finally brought down by the Falcons at their 40 yard line.

Owen, Terry, and I were so busy celebrating that we didn't even notice what was happening on the field until someone called out, "I think he's hurt." We turned to see Don still lying on his back, barely moving his feet, and grimacing in pain. Austin was kneeling over him, his hand on the running back's chest, trying to keep him still until the trainers arrived.

In a show of solidarity, a handful of Falcons gathered around, taking a knee in prayer as the entire stadium went silent.

We watched with everyone else as the trainers were talking to Don. He remained on the ground for several moments as Austin, Wesley, and Wickie looked on. Then with the help of one of the trainers, Don sat up, stretched his back, and rose to his feet, drawing thunderous applause from the crowd and an enormous sigh of relief from everyone on the Vipers bench. The trainers stayed with the still-wobbly running back until they reached the sidelines, where he was met by his coach with a grateful hug.

I later asked one of the trainers what had happened. He just laughed. "He's going to be fine. We headed out there thinking we'd need to assess him for a possible concussion, but all he kept asking was, 'Did it work? Did he catch it?' As soon as we told him how the play ended, he high-fived both of us and then collapsed back to the ground, grimacing from the pain in his ribs—we're pretty sure they're cracked."

As the other trainer helped Don onto the cart to take him back to the locker room for X-rays, the team turned their attention to the field. Wickie had gained forty-five yards, putting the Vipers on the verge of field goal territory. Joe wanted to get closer than the fifty-seven yards they now faced.

Not wanting to risk an interception that would end our chances, Whit called two straight running plays, which netted just four yards. There were only six seconds left in regulation. We'd either win or lose on Patrick Kingsby's kick.

Patrick lined up his attempt, and as expected, just before the ball was snapped, the Falcons called a time-out to give the kicker a little more time to think things over. Off to my left, I heard a voice say, "I can't watch."

I looked over to see Terry sink to the ground, sitting on the floor of the box beneath the window level, eyes closed, fingers steepled across the top of his head.

Now that's not very judicial looking, I thought.

Along the Vipers sideline, some players formed a line in unity, while others stood up on the benches to get a better view. Despite the pressure of the situation, the conditions in the dome were perfect for a kicker—no wind, and the footing was ideal. The snap and the hold were perfect. The crowd held its collective breath as the ball left Patrick's foot and just cleared a rushing Falcon's outstretched wingspan. It seemed to float in the air forever, gently losing altitude until it *barely* cleared the crossbar. As the officials raised their hands over their heads in unison, signaling that the kick was good, the Vipers sideline exploded, launching its players out onto the field to mob the elated Patrick on the 40 yard line.

Against all conceivable odds, the Vipers were going to the Super Bowl!

JUST THE BEGINNING

THE BALL BOUNCED ACROSS THE LAWN, hit a bump, and changed course.

"Stay in front of it, Jason," Justin called out as his little brother scrambled to get back into the ball's path.

It was another picture-perfect February day in Tampa, and I was out in the backyard watching the boys play. Jason was just starting his first year of Little League, and as a now-seasoned pro, Justin was helping him get—as Justin phrased it—"game ready."

As the ball continued to roll, Jason reached down and scooped it up with the tip of his glove, just off to his right.

"Try not to play it off to the side if you can help it," Justin called out.

"He sounds just like you." I turned, surprised to see Terry standing right behind me.

"Hey, Terry!" I reached over and shook his hand. "I wasn't expecting to see you again so soon." Lauren and I had just seen Terry and his wife two weeks before in Orlando when we sat down to dinner after the Vipers' Super Bowl victory parade.

Terry smiled, tilting his head a bit to shade his eyes from the sun. "Well, I was in the area, so I thought I'd stop by. Lauren let me in." He nodded back toward the house.

I raised my eyebrows. "She did?"

"Yeah." He looked down at the ground and laughed. "Considering how long we held you hostage last season, I was a little surprised she opened the door."

"You and me both," I said, smiling. "Oh, by the way, I heard the stadium referendum passed with flying colors. Congratulations! How's Owen feeling about everything?"

"Oh, he's on cloud nine! I have to tell you, Tony, I've known Owen for going on twenty years now. I've watched him close some of the biggest business deals on record, and I have *never* seen him as excited as he is right now. Seriously, he's like a new man."

"Well, that's fantastic, Terry. I'm really happy to hear it."

We stood and watched as Justin smacked another grounder across the lawn, and this time, Jason got right in front of it, catching it in the webbing.

"That's what I'm talking about!" Justin called out.

"Oh wow, you're right," I laughed. "He does sound like me."

Terry cast a cautious glance over his shoulder. "So, any chance I could convince you to stick around for another season? We've got a lot to build on."

I shook my head. "Sorry, Terry, but now I really am officially retired. Besides, you don't need me anymore. Your organization has found its SOUL. Look at Joe. A year ago, all he cared about was winning the Super Bowl, no matter what it cost or what he had to do to get there. Now he just wants to be the best coach, the best leader, and the best example he possibly can—for his players, his coaching staff, and everyone who comes after him.

"And look at Whit and DC," I continued. "They used to be at each other's throats—angry, bitter, resentful."

"That's for sure," Terry said.

"Look at them now. I don't expect they'll ever become best friends, but at least they've figured out that the team benefits more—in fact, *they* benefit more—when they look for ways to complement each other as opposed to competing."

Terry nodded.

"Gym knows the kind of players to avoid down the road," I continued, "and the kind who are worth investing in."

"I suppose you're right," Terry agreed. "Who would have guessed that Wesley Robinson would wind up being a more valuable asset than Fred Ashford?"

"Well, my friend," I pointed out, "I think you'll find that when you have a clear set of values driving your decisions, you don't really have to *guess*. And between Austin, Louis, Don, Wickie, and Wesley, you've got a solid core of leaders committed to maintaining a culture of selflessness, ownership, and unity. And that's going to bring you sustained success for years to come."

Terry shot me a concerned look. "But what happens when those guys leave?"

"That won't matter," I explained. "The culture has been established. Everyone from Owen to the coaching staff to the practice squad is modeling and promoting the principles of SOUL. You all just need to keep working at it—it does need continued attention, of course," I reminded him.

Terry rubbed the back of his neck and paused to watch Justin knock another grounder Jason's way, then turned back to me. "I wonder what would have happened if things didn't work out the way they did—if we hadn't reached the playoffs."

"Don't you see, Terry? It doesn't matter. You've got an organization full of selfless individuals," I explained, "who each perform to the best of their ability and are all unified around a purpose larger and more important than any ring or trophy could ever be.

"The Vipers' success is no longer limited to or defined just by wins and losses," I continued. "It's measured by the positive impact you're having on one another, the fans, and the community. And as long as your end goal is to do what's right, and honest, and good for the benefit of all involved, then no matter what happens, you're always going to come out on top."

Terry shook his head and smiled. "I can't argue with you there." Then he paused for a second, threw up his hands, and said, "Well . . . all right then. I guess that's it. Tony, I guess you're fired." His face widened into a smile.

"You're the judge," I said, grinning.

"Hey, Dad!" Justin called from the yard. "Can you please throw us a few pitches?"

I turned to Terry. "Care to shag some flies?"

He just smiled and started rolling up his sleeves. "I'd love to."

PART V

Putting the Principles into Practice

Finding Your SOUL

When he was asked what made the Pittsburgh Steelers such standouts in the 1970s, Coach Chuck Noll said, "The most important thing we had . . . was the ability to work together."

Of course, if working together were easy, there wouldn't be so much written about it, and every team would be wildly successful. So what separates the truly great teams from the mediocre ones? As you've just seen, it basically boils down to four simple yet highly effective principles—selflessness, ownership, unity, and larger purpose—which together form what I like to call the SOUL of a team.

In all my years of coaching and working with teams, both athletic and corporate, I've yet to encounter a successful team that doesn't practice these principles. Simply put, a team that has SOUL can and will accomplish far more than one that doesn't. It's what gives a team its identity, its focus, its drive, and its sense of being. It's what inspires individual members to do their best and to come together as one to achieve something as a group that wouldn't be possible by any one person.

I used a fictional football team to illustrate the principles of SOUL, but I can assure you that these principles will hold true for any business, nonprofit, church, or other type of organization. The key—as was evidenced by the Vipers—is getting everyone on your team to commit.

Normally, change happens from the top down. But as we've just seen, change makers can exist at any level. In fact, sometimes change takes place from the bottom up. In the case of the Vipers, Wesley Robinson, the soft-spoken rookie, helped institute change on the team long before Owen, the team's owner, got on board. The point is, your position, title, or personality type doesn't matter. It makes no difference whether you are a CEO or an administrative assistant. As Coach Noll also used to say, "Everybody is important—even when you think you might not be." Great leaders set the standard, model excellence, and hold others accountable—and that needs to happen at every level for a team to be successful in the long haul.

Now that you've seen how the Vipers found their SOUL, I invite you to consider how to strengthen your own team by embracing selflessness, ownership, and unity to achieve a larger purpose and to use SOUL as a benchmark to help get back on course if your team falters.

In addition to fleshing out each principle a bit more in the pages that follow, I provide some diagnostic questions to help you assess how well you are doing in each area, both individually and as an organization, as well as some suggested action steps you can take to help your team achieve peak performance.

A final word before you read on: Most people who know me understand that my Christian faith plays a significant role in my life. So it's no coincidence that the four principles you've just been introduced to and are about to learn more about are actually rooted in Scripture. Even the acronym SOUL is based on one of my favorite verses:

> What do you benefit if you gain the whole world but lose your own soul?
> MATTHEW 16:26

It was Owen's acknowledgment of this timeless truth that ultimately served as the catalyst for change in his heart, and I hope it will inspire you as well.

Good luck and God bless.

—Tony Dungy

SELFLESSNESS

Definition: Putting individual needs aside for the good of the team

In 2007, just before my final season as a head coach, the Colts drafted Anthony Gonzalez, a wide receiver from Ohio State. Because he wouldn't complete his studies until June, Anthony was unable to make off-season practices and minicamp.

Not wanting his new teammate to miss out on this training, Peyton Manning drove three hours to Columbus twice a week so he could spend an hour going over the playbook with Anthony and another hour and a half throwing to him. Peyton then made the three-hour drive back to Indianapolis. In other words, Peyton—a multiple MVP award winner—devoted about seventeen hours a week to helping a rookie wide receiver learn his role. He willingly sacrificed his own time because that's what the Colts needed to be successful. This, to me, is an excellent illustration of selflessness.

In the fable, we see several players and coaches model self-less behavior, though perhaps the most striking is when Don Buerkle hurls himself in front of Austin to prevent a sack, buying the quarterback just enough time to complete the pass that leads to the game-winning field goal.

Getting team members to put themselves somewhere other than first can be a challenge. After all, it often conflicts with a natural desire for self-advancement. And if your team is struggling, your first thought may be, *I'd better protect myself and do what's best for me, because at the end of the day, that's going to be the way I get ahead.* As one player recently told me, "Being on a bad team is the first step to being out of the league." The irony, however, is that putting your interests aside for the good of the team ultimately benefits both you and those with whom you work.

Be careful, though, that you don't confuse selflessness with false humility or being a doormat. Truly selfless team members are confident in their own abilities. But instead of just using those abilities to their own benefit, they see them as gifts that can be used to help others. When Wickie took the time to teach Wesley Robinson his patented swim move so he could get off the line faster, Wickie not only made the team stronger but also created a second passing threat, which actually helped him, too. When the apostle Paul was advising an early church on how it could thrive despite great challenges, he said, "Be humble, thinking of others as better than yourselves. Don't look out only for your own interests, but take an interest in others, too" (Philippians 2:3-4).

Likewise, being selfless doesn't mean you must always put your needs and wants last, and you certainly shouldn't ignore them. Paul wasn't telling the Philippian church to disregard their own needs but to look for opportunities to help others, even as they were faithful to their own responsibilities. We saw this play itself out in the fable when DC, Stan, and Whit haggled over their final roster spots. While everyone had a dream pick, all of them were willing to compromise to make sure the whole team benefited, as opposed to just their segment of the team.

The Lord has put passions and dreams not only into your heart but also into the hearts of your fellow team members. Those dreams and desires are important. The people who hold them are important too. You can have a hand in helping others flourish. The payoff? When you are selfless, you'll become part of something bigger and more successful than yourself alone. And you'll earn the respect of your teammates.

I remember a time when the Colts were preparing for the college draft and needed to choose between two defensive players. One was big, strong, and dominant on the field. The other had great speed but was undersized. Both were exceptional college players, and we rated them almost equally in terms of physical talent.

Yet we had some questions about the first player's attitude and commitment to follow through. So we brought in three of his college teammates and asked each of them, "If we brought you here, which of your teammates would you want to have on our team as well?" These three recommended several teammates, but none of them named the player we were considering. That told us all we needed to know. We ended up drafting the second player, and he was a good choice.

Hard workers—people who are constantly seeking to improve, yet who are also willing to allow their individual goals to take a backseat or be revised altogether for the good of the whole—are exactly the type of people you want on your team.

No matter your role or position, you must be selfless and realize that it's not all about you. You are a part of something bigger.

Diagnosis

1. When was the last time you put a team member's needs ahead of your own? Or when one or more of your team members put another's needs before their own? How did that impact you? The other person? Your team?

2. Do your actions reflect a greater desire to get ahead personally or to advance your team's interests? Explain.

3. How easy is it for you to overlook a real or perceived slight by a fellow team member?

4. Does your team make it easy or difficult to put another person's needs above your own? Why?

5. Does *sacrifice* always mean meeting a team member's desires? Why or why not?

6. How does your age, seniority, or position on a team affect the way you serve others?

7. If you lead a team, how do you model selflessness? What might you do to encourage this virtue in others?

Development

How you can become a more selfless team player

1. To be selfless, you must first recognize your own value. Summarize the skills, experience, and character traits that you contribute to your team. If you've never identified

your strengths, consider using StrengthsFinder[1] or another personality-assessment tool to identify those areas where you can most contribute to others.

2. To be selfless, you must also be humble, desiring to put the needs of others above your own. To put this into practice, look for an opportunity to encourage or help someone on your team, even if it inconveniences you.

3. As Sir Isaac Newton said, "If I have seen further it is by standing on the shoulders of giants." Make a list of the "giants" in your life (not the ones in New York!), those whose sacrifices helped you get where you are now. Take a few minutes to call or write to let them know what their selflessness has meant for you.

4. Remember the impact that basic courtesies—saying thank you, acknowledging a compliment, or letting someone go ahead of you—can make on your own attitude as well as on the other person's.

OWNERSHIP

Definition: Fulfilling your role by learning it thoroughly and by consistently giving 100 percent

Though it sounds simple, owning your role requires you to be present, positive, proactive, and prepared.

Even now, the players who stand out to me are the ones who show up faithfully every day, ready to work hard and give their all to whatever task is in front of them. They exemplify one of Scripture's definitions of faithfulness: "Whatever you do, work at it with all your heart" (Colossians 3:23, NIV). When it matters most, they come through. Remember Wesley Robinson's dogged determination to learn his position? Despite racking up a number of rookie mistakes early in the season, the inexperienced wide receiver asked questions, watched lots of game film, and treated every practice like it counted as much as a game—and to him it did.

On the other hand, I've seen players fail to improve because they assume the team will never depend on them. At times these players—maybe not stars but solid backups—don't work very hard or study the game plan. After all, they don't expect to play on game day, or their roles at the moment are not what they want them to be. When they do play, the results are predictable: They generally fail to produce, sometimes even costing their teams a win.

Don Shula, Chuck Noll, John Wooden, and countless other coaches long preached about—and personally practiced—the importance of staying on top of the details. Their understanding reflects the words of another great team builder, Jesus: "If you are faithful in little things, you will be faithful in large ones. But if you are dishonest in little things, you won't be honest with greater responsibilities" (Luke 16:10).

Those who own their roles not only are present but also remain positive. A few years ago, James Robertson, a fifty-six-year-old factory worker from Detroit, made national news after his city newspaper featured a report about his forty-six-mile daily job commute. It wasn't merely the overall length of the trip that caught the media's attention but the fact that Robertson had to walk about twenty of those miles. (He rode a bus when he could, which covered the rest.) His attendance record? So good that his supervisor said, "I set our attendance standard by this man."[2]

Though Robertson couldn't afford to replace the car that

had died a decade before, he said he never considered not showing up for work. He not only took pride in his job running an injection-molding machine but also said he enjoyed working with his teammates: "We're like a family."[3]

A suburban banker had seen Robertson walking along the side of the road many times as he was driving to his own job. One day he happened to park and get out of his car just as Robertson passed by. They struck up a conversation, and eventually the banker shared Robertson's story, which eventually was picked up by a reporter. Robertson inspired so many people that a GoFundMe account was set up in his name, and a local car dealership even donated a new vehicle to him.

What I love about the story is Robertson's positive outlook: Even if the banker had never stopped to talk with him, I have no doubt Robertson would be continuing to make the daily trek to the job he loved. He was present and positive every single day.

Another defining trait of people who own their roles is their willingness to be proactive and prepare. They take the long view. For example, employees holding entry-level positions in a sales department may spend their days fielding phone calls and e-mails, organizing travel for sales reps, and scanning documents. Those with the most potential don't just settle for getting by; rather, they recognize they're responsible for making good first impressions on potential customers, ensuring efficiency as the sales reps cover large territories, and maintaining accurate records.

Owning their role doesn't mean these inexperienced workers will never leave to pursue other opportunities. But it does mean they remain focused on giving their very best *right where they are*. They are also proactive, readying themselves for future opportunities. That may mean asking to accompany a senior rep on sales calls or to sit in on phone calls with clients. They may take continuing-education classes online in the evenings.

They are fully present to what is in front of them while preparing for greater responsibilities or roles that may be of more interest to them.

If you are a team leader, be sure to encourage those who are embracing their roles and look for opportunities to help them develop further by stretching them beyond their comfort zones.

One way I did this as a coach was by organizing what we called the "Mock Game" before the start of a new season. I orchestrated much of the play so the team could practice different situations that might come up only once a year. I also wanted to give the other coaches a chance to get a feel for calling and adjusting plays before the first preseason game. But rather than splitting the teams up evenly, I put myself and the special teams coach in charge of the team made up of backup players; the rest of the coaching staff took the starters.

I organized the Mock Game this way for two reasons. One, I wanted to see the young players and backups handle the mental adversity of going against the starters. Who would be able to perform well even when their team was outmanned? Who would go out there and do their jobs no matter who their opponents were?

Second, because I appointed myself the referee, I could create adversity with bad—even downright unfair—calls. After all, nothing the players faced during the season could be more unfair than the referee coaching the opposing team. Meanwhile, the special teams coach would design gadget plays such as onside kicks, fake punts, and fake field goals. As expected, the team made up of starters usually won, but it was never as easy as they thought it would be. Afterward, we were able to talk about playing as heavy favorites, playing as underdogs, and reacting appropriately in the face of the unexpected, such as replay reversals.

The Mock Game was a practice I devised to help every player fully own his role. But that was just one day. Those who accomplished the most were players who prepared, stayed present and positive, and were proactive each and every day.

Diagnosis

1. How invested are you in your position on a typical day? On a scale of 1 (very low) to 5 (very high), rate yourself according to how present, prepared, positive, and proactive you are.

2. Recognizing that every player is important, how would you describe the contribution you make to your team?

3. In what areas might you be coasting in your current position? Why?

    a. If you are bored, how might you challenge yourself?

    b. If you feel stuck, how might you get the help you need or prepare yourself for more responsibility?

    c. If you are overwhelmed, how might you get the support you need to ensure all parts of your role are covered well?

4. Do you consider any parts of your role "beneath you"? How might embracing all aspects of your role benefit you and your organization?

5. What bad habits, distractions, or excuses may be keeping you from working with all your heart?

Development

How you can strengthen your team by more fully owning your role

1. Learn to be present on the job each day, always on the lookout for new things to learn and new ways to contribute to your team.

2. We are urged to "be thankful in all circumstances" (1 Thessalonians 5:18), just as James Robertson was. Are there ways in which you need to be more positive? It may take some creative thinking.

3. Be honest about any barriers within yourself that are keeping you from giving your best each day.

4. Study your job description (or create one if it doesn't exist in your setting). Determine one area in which you might focus on improving.

5. Seek a mentor—someone you look up to who may be ahead of you in your role and whose work, character, and positivity you admire.

6. Don't be afraid to admit to needing help or direction in specific areas of your life.

7. Own up to your mistakes; view them as opportunities to grow rather than as blunders to hide.

8. If you are a team leader, help your team own their roles by looking for ways to acknowledge their contributions and encourage their continued growth.

UNITY

Definition: Understanding and rallying around your team's mission, philosophy, and culture through open communication and positive conflict resolution

Have you ever tried to push through a door that was designed to be pulled open? No matter how hard you push, you won't get through it. Likewise, a team whose members are pursuing different objectives or who rebel against the culture will never succeed. In fact, a team that isn't unified and headed in the same direction isn't much of a team at all. It's simply a collection of individuals.

No wonder the apostle Peter, when writing to a group of early Christians facing intense opposition, encouraged them to remember these principles: "All of you should be of one mind. Sympathize with each other. Love each other as brothers and sisters. Be tenderhearted, and keep a humble attitude" (1 Peter 3:8). Unity requires consideration among team members, but it begins with holding a common purpose.

Note that someone can bring disunity without being completely at odds with what the team is trying to accomplish. Often just as detrimental, and harder to spot, is the person whose purpose is just slightly off from the team's. Little by little, over time, the team may find itself well off course as a result.

The Vipers couldn't excel when Whit, the offensive coordinator, and DC, the defensive coordinator, were too busy looking out for themselves to worry about the whole team. Likewise, Joe was so preoccupied with how to keep his head coaching job that he barely noticed that Whit and DC were at each other's throats. When team players aren't committed to advancing the interests of their organization and one another, they cannot generate the momentum needed for high achievement. Once the Vipers coaching staff began to work toward the same purpose, however, everything changed.

I faced a similar challenge in 1996 when I started with the Buccaneers, who were in a streak of thirteen losing seasons. I knew that creating a winning culture would begin by casting a vision of excellence and high achievement. I had to establish a championship mind-set, devise a plan to meet our goals, and then make sure we were all about that.

I raised the bar during my very first meeting with the players. I told them, "We don't want to just be good. We don't simply want to break our streak. We want to win Super Bowls and be the best, and here's what it's going to take."

Then I laid out the many sacrifices we would have to make to reach our objectives. I explained that we would need to act like champions everywhere—during off-season conditioning, in our meeting rooms, in the community, in being accountable to ourselves in ways that might not even seem to matter. "We're going to be winners in everything we do," I said, "and that will help us win on the field."

Of course, I had to back that up through my own conduct and by holding everyone to a high standard. I also had to bring key players like Warren Sapp on board. After outlining my expectations to Warren, I reminded him that the other players were going to follow him. If he led in the direction our team had set, we could be champions. If he led them in an opposite direction, we would be held back.

To his credit, Warren told me, "I'm not going to be perfect, but you just draw the line. If you draw the line, I'll toe it. I'll never cross it. I'll be right on the line but never cross it." And he lived up to that promise.

New England Patriots head coach Bill Belichick has mastered

the concept of unity. He values the culture so much that he not only helps his players understand it but also helps them discover how they can be productive and fit into the landscape. As a result, even players who've had problems elsewhere are likely to conclude, *You know what? I've sometimes bucked the system in other places, but I'm going to accept the culture here.*

This played out for the Vipers when Austin called out Wickie for not staying behind to sign autographs for the fans, and again when Joe made the difficult decision to sit Don after he refused to get on board with the team's overall plan. Once the team culture is set and you've got buy-in and support from within, rogue players tend to stand out like sore thumbs, and it becomes extremely difficult to buck the system.

Granted, rallying behind a team's mission doesn't mean you should never question a decision you don't understand. As a member of any team, your opinion matters. You can't truly get behind a philosophy or strategy that doesn't make sense to you. In fact, by voicing your questions and concerns respectfully but directly, you may be helping to build a more unified team.

That's exactly what Jeff Saturday did not long after the Colts won the Super Bowl in 2007. As we were planning our off-season training program, Jeff came to me after talking with some of the other veteran players. He pointed out that since we'd played four or five extra weeks into the postseason for several years straight, perhaps that year we didn't need as much off-season work. He made his point respectfully, and I promised to consider it. When I did, I realized his case was a good one. As a result, we came up with a plan that provided the rookies and younger guys with the work they needed while reducing the wear and tear on the older guys, who between postseason games and off-season practices had put in about sixteen extra weeks over the past three years. I was grateful Jeff had possessed the confidence to come to me and present the veteran players' concerns, and they were grateful I had listened.

Of course, my decisions didn't always please everyone. My objective, however, was to discuss and dissect ideas together. At some point, though, I had to say, "Okay, *this* is what we're going to do." I then expected my staff to present that plan to the team and tell them, "This is the best plan we could come up with. Now let's do it."

How leaders communicate is also important. Body language and tone can either build cooperation and a sense that you are all in it together or create an us-versus-them environment that leads to friction and mistrust.

That doesn't mean you can avoid all disagreement simply by remaining positive. Even the strongest team will not remain unified if it doesn't deal with conflict head-on. While the disputes between Whit and DC early in the season didn't contribute to a sense of unity, their eventual ability to communicate constructively through conflict was an important part of the Vipers' building—and maintaining—a unified organization. Once DC shared his opinion, Joe and Whit slowly began to address his concerns by adjusting their own strategies. The result? The Vipers were much more unified than they would have been if Joe had merely sought to quell the dissension and sweep it under the rug, unresolved.

Imagine for a moment what would have happened if DC had allowed his frustration to build to the boiling point without sharing his feelings. We've all seen it—employees who swallow their tongues and pride for the sake of "keeping the peace" (and as often as not, further undermining unity by privately airing their grievances). A simple lack of complaints doesn't necessarily speak to unity, nor does it help the organization maximize its performance. Remember that unity doesn't mean everyone must think or act alike. It doesn't even mean that we need to treat everyone in exactly the same way to be fair. Unity simply means keeping the same goals and end result in mind.

Do you still wonder whether unity can really strengthen your team? Let me illustrate the principle by sharing one of my proudest moments. Oddly enough, it came at my dad's funeral, when I learned during one of the eulogies that Wilbur Dungy had been a member of the Tuskegee Airmen. This program, launched by the Army Air Corps in 1941, was the first to train African Americans to serve as officers and pilots. Despite many Americans' opposition and skepticism to the idea that black pilots could fight as effectively as their fellow officers, more than one thousand Tuskegee airmen completed the rigorous training program. Eventually the Tuskegee pilots flew more than fifteen thousand missions in Europe and North Africa during World War II. United in their desire to serve their country alongside other Americans, the Tuskegee Airmen helped win the war. Perhaps more significantly, their many successes were key to ending segregation of America's armed services in 1948.[4]

Unity amid diversity—another key to the success of an organization.

Diagnosis

1. How open are your team members to giving and receiving input from one another?

2. How do you promote and support your organization's vision to others?

3. How comfortable are you in engaging in conflict when you believe the team's mission is at stake?

4. In your position, what are some ways you can hold others accountable in a respectful way?

5. Are you involved in any harmful practices—such as back-stabbing, complaining, or holding on to grudges—that might be affecting your team's unity? What steps might you take to correct these counterproductive reactions?

6. Do you agree that diversity does not preclude unity within an organization? Why or why not?

7. As a team member, how readily do you accept the decisions of your superiors?

8. If you are a leader, what steps are you taking to promote unity among your teammates?

Development
How you can become a team player who promotes unity

1. Commit your team mission statement to memory.

2. Look for ways to communicate that mission statement to others—both through words and actions.

3. Encourage those you see contributing to the unity of the team.

4. Be willing to give input when you're asked to do so.

5. Don't hold a grudge if team leaders ultimately decide to go in a different direction.

6. Learn to engage in constructive conflict. Communicate in a manner that's helpful.

7. Look for ways to celebrate the successes of your team.

LARGER PURPOSE

Definition: Contributing to the wider community in a lasting and significant way

About a year after joining the Minnesota Vikings as defensive coordinator in 1992, I began meeting every Thursday morning with Tom Lamphere, the team's chaplain. At his suggestion, we began studying the Old Testament book of Nehemiah.

Tom felt I had the potential to become a head coach one day, and he thought that by learning and applying the leadership lessons in Nehemiah, I would be preparing myself for increasing responsibilities.

My studies with Tom were so significant that, when a replica of my locker was displayed at the Pro Football Hall of Fame, it contained a Bible, opened to the book of Nehemiah, just in front of my game ball from Super Bowl XLI. To me, it signified the way God guides and leads those who commit to following his own larger purpose.

I've come to see that Nehemiah was a leader who exemplified SOUL. Few men demonstrated greater selflessness. An exile who'd become a trusted assistant to a powerful king, Nehemiah gave it all up for the opportunity to return home and oversee the rebuilding of the city walls—critical to keeping the nation's enemies out. And there were many.

Nehemiah was not only a selfless leader, but he also took ownership. After he'd spent months praying about and preparing for his adventure, Nehemiah finally received the king's permission to return home. He then planned and led the entire rebuilding effort—from recruiting overseers and laborers to providing for the workers' physical needs to anticipating and overcoming obstacles. In just fifty-two days, they rebuilt the entire wall, which scholars say was about two and a half miles long and forty feet high.

When he first arrived in Jerusalem, Nehemiah laid out a vision for the project, helping the people still living in Jerusalem understand how their country could be renewed and offering evidence that the Lord had opened this opportunity for them. When the outside opposition became more intense and his countrymen's enthusiasm waned, Nehemiah devised a way for the work to continue, even as he strengthened their defenses. He kept a sometimes hopeless and harassed people unified.

Although *L* is the last letter in the acronym SOUL, everything we've discussed springs from it. It's what drove Nehemiah to leave a high position in the king's court to rally a demoralized nation and help revitalize not only their city but also their relationship to God. In our story, it's the reason Wesley Robinson organized Robinson's Road Warriors, providing at-risk kids a chance to visit new cities and learn from mentors. It's why the suspended Don Buerkle voluntarily stepped up to help his backup become a better blocker.

It's also why former Pittsburgh Steelers owner Art Rooney never moved out of inner-city Pittsburgh and why he expected his players and staff to give back in tangible ways to the community. It's the reason Lauren and I were drawn to Indianapolis when Colts owner Jim Irsay told us his priority was to build a team that emphasized character and family and would do so in a way that would benefit the surrounding metropolitan area and the state.

Larger purpose imbues meaning into everything we do. In that way, it's *primus inter pares*: first among equals. That larger purpose must be something that will capture the imagination of team members, no matter their roles or positions within the organization. It must be something they can rally around. At the same time, it must not merely be a lofty ideal; instead, it has to lead to tangible acts and relationships that create opportunities and offer hope to others. Without a larger purpose, it's almost impossible to build a sustainable S, O, and U.

I'm not the first to notice this, not by a long shot. Many contemporary business leaders emphasize one's larger purpose—even if they don't use that language. Simon Sinek talks about "knowing your why,"[5] while Stephen Covey urges us to put "first things first."[6] Jim Collins and Jerry Porras say the *why* matters "more than profits,"[7] and Jon Gordon talks of having a "greater purpose"[8] to leave a legacy. Countless organizations, including Family First, All Pro Dad, and Impact for Living, three organizations I support, wrestle with their impact—the *why* that drives their work. The *why* should always be the first consideration and step before the *how*.

On a visit to Argentina, Blake Mycoskie was struck by the sight of many children running around without shoes because their families couldn't afford them. His company, TOMS, was born from his idea of giving one pair of shoes to an impoverished child for every pair of shoes sold. The company has not only given away more than two million pairs of shoes to children in Argentina, Rwanda, Ethiopia, and other countries but has also since used its "One for One" business model to expand into eyewear and apparel.

In his book on entrepreneurship, Mycoskie notes, "Conscious capitalism is about more than simply making money. . . . It's about creating a successful business that also connects supporters to something that matters to them and that has great impact in the world."[9]

The reason that maximizing profits or winning a championship makes such a lousy purpose on its own is that neither lasts. Coach Noll told his players, "Football should be important— it's your job. But don't make it your life." As gratifying as our time in the NFL might be, he said, at some point every one of us would have to leave it. If we had placed all our meaning, significance, and joy in the game, we would inevitably be disappointed. A purpose without meaning will leave us—leave our souls—empty. And as Jesus asked, "Is anything worth more than your soul?" (Matthew 16:26).

Although the Vipers won the Super Bowl, the story would have worked equally well had they lost their final game. In fact, considering how many variables—from a bad call to a game-ending injury—can cut a great team's season short, that ending might have been more believable. But the key to this story isn't whether the Vipers won or lost the Super Bowl. That's why I didn't spend any time talking about the game itself or the victory parade that followed. The real victory for the Vipers isn't the Lombardi Trophy; it's the fact they finally came together as a single, unified team composed of selfless players who engaged in every game to the best of their ability, looked for opportunities to help one another, and were driven by a common purpose greater than any ring, title, or trophy.

I wanted to show what can happen when a floundering team comes together around a core philosophy that guides their decision-making, shapes their relationships, and influences their conduct. Most important, I wanted to show how rallying around a larger purpose can give a team a vibrancy and sense of worth it wouldn't otherwise have.

Because the Vipers achieved this, they will be positioned for success not just for a single game but year after year as well. That's the ultimate goal of SOUL—lasting and meaningful success.

So how do you determine the larger purpose for yourself or your team? Just as I explained to Terry Hodges in the story, I also can't tell you what your larger purpose should be. That's up to you and your team. Think long-term by asking yourself what kind of legacy you want to leave and how you can impact others' lives—maybe even for eternity. Then look for ways in which your larger purpose can impact the work you do and the way you do it. Even if it's not perfect at first blush, press ahead. I guarantee that taking the time to uncover and refine your larger purpose—either for your team or for your own life—is well worth it.

I know I have gotten where I am only because so many people—from my parents to fellow players and coaches—made influencing and supporting me part of their larger purpose. And centering my larger purpose on other people—recognizing that God created them to last forever and has a good plan for them too—gives each new day meaning and joy.

I want the same for you. Find your SOUL, and you will create something bigger and longer lasting than you have ever imagined.

Diagnosis

1. Can you define your team's larger purpose? If so, how would you explain it to others?

2. If you can't articulate it, ask your team's leaders for help in defining it.

3. What attracts people to work for your team? What does that reveal about its deeper purpose?

4. How does your larger purpose fit into the legacy you hope to leave someday?

5. In what ways does your team honor and support others?

6. If your organization were to cease to exist tomorrow, what impact, if any, would that have on your community?

7. Does your life have a larger purpose that gives it meaning? Explain.

Development
How you can find meaning and significance through a larger purpose

1. Take a few minutes to consider the needs of the wider community that your organization is a part of.

2. Decide as a team the unique contribution you can make to your community.

3. As a team, strategize on the first steps needed to impact those you have decided to help.

4. Seek your community's input on how you can provide even more value to those around you.

Group Discussion Guide

PART I: THE PROBLEM

1. Tony tells Owen that "there are ways for organizations to define success other than a Super Bowl win" (page 16). Is there a pinnacle in your field or industry? What are some other ways your team or organization would define success? How unified are team members around a definition of success?

2. During his initial conversation with Joe, Tony cautions against using injuries or bad calls as excuses for not winning. He explains that "the difference between playoff-caliber teams and everyone else is the ability to stay the course regardless of the 'uncontrollables'" (page 20). What are some of the uncontrollables that impact your team's success rate? What safeguards might you put in place to protect yourself against them, or—at the very least—limit their impact?

3. What is the leading cause of tension among the Vipers coaching staff? What factors within your organization prevent your team from functioning as smoothly and effectively as possible?

4. Tony tells Terry that "what you invest in now will determine the kind of returns you see in the future" (page 54). Discuss how this adage might apply to your team/ organization. What are you investing in? What should you be investing in?

PART II: THE PLAN

5. Terry, Gym, and Joe are frustrated because the team isn't responding to Tony's pep talk about playing with "SOUL." What is the difference between having a mission statement and implementing that mission?

6. To help them see beyond the mentality that winning is everything, Tony challenges Gym, Terry, and Joe to articulate *why* they want to win. What motivates your team to do what you do?

7. Gym points out that although Dan Marino has never won a Super Bowl, he is still considered one of the greatest quarterbacks to ever play the game. Discuss how your definition of success can expand or limit the way you view both your own accomplishments and those of others.

8. What specific qualities were Joe, Gym, and Terry looking for when selecting the trio of players (Austin, Louis, and Wesley) to serve as team leaders (see pages 93–98)? What qualities does your organization or team look for in potential leaders?

PART III: THE PROGRESS

9. When Wickie skips out on the autograph session after practice at the high school football field, Austin and Louis call him out in front of the rest of the team. How does being confronted about poor behavior differ when it comes from a colleague as opposed to a boss? Which is more impactful? Why?

10. Tony shares one of his favorite quotes from Chuck Noll: "Every player is important . . . but *no one* is indispensable" (page 134). Do you agree or disagree? Why?

11. Because Whit tries to run up the score to impress his former team, the Texans, the Vipers suffer an upset. Later Tony points out that since the situation might ultimately result in greater unity for Whit and DC, the Vipers may have benefited more from the loss than they would have from a win. Discuss a time when a perceived setback actually helped your team/organization move forward.

12. Discuss the impact that sitting Don Buerkle for two games has on the players and the coaching staff.

PART IV: THE PAYOFF

13. As the regular season draws to a close, we see major changes in Wickie's and Don's attitudes. In what ways has each grown as a player and a person since the preseason, and to what, specifically, do you attribute these changes?

14. Discuss Owen's change of heart on the stadium deal. What do you feel was the tipping point for him? Where do you see generosity within your team or organization? What effect does it have?

15. Though we don't get to see it, what do you think Joe stresses to the players in his pregame Super Bowl pep talk? How effective are pep talks, if there are any, in your organization?

16. What if the Vipers had lost the Super Bowl? In what respects might they still consider their season a success?

VIPERS PERSONNEL

Character List

Owen Joyce—Vipers owner

Terry Hodges—team president

Gym McKenzie—general manager

Joe Webster—head coach

Whit Jansen—offensive coordinator

Dennis "DC" Coleman—defensive coordinator

Stan Taylor—special teams coordinator

Wilson Grady—wide receivers coach

Scott Pendleton—director of college scouting

Mark King—head of marketing department

Perry Richards—head of public relations

Stacy Banks—salary cap administrator, or "capologist"

Austin Quarles—starting quarterback and team captain

Wickie Ariet—starting wide receiver

Don Buerkle—starting running back

Louis Blackstock—starting linebacker

Patrick Kingsby—placekicker

Larry Bannister—veteran linebacker

Wesley Robinson—backup wide receiver

Brendan Quinlan—backup quarterback

Cornelius Brooks—backup corner

Thomas Dorr—backup running back

NOTES

FINDING YOUR SOUL
1. Tom Rath, *StrengthsFinder 2.0*, (New York: Gallup, 2007).
2. Bill Laitner, "Heart and Sole: Detroiter Walks 21 Miles in Work Commute," *Detroit Free Press*, February 10, 2015, https://www.freep.com/story/news /local/michigan/oakland/2015/01/31/detroit-commuting-troy-rochester-hills -smart-ddot-ubs-banker-woodward-buses-transit/22660785/.
3. Ibid.
4. History, "Tuskegee Airmen," accessed July 22, 2018, https://www.history.com /topics/world-war-ii/tuskegee-airmen.
5. Simon Sinek with David Mead and Peter Docker, *Find Your Why: A Practical Guide for Discovering Purpose for You and Your Team* (New York: Portfolio / Penguin, 2017).
6. Stephen R. Covey with A. Roger and Rebecca R. Merrill, *First Things First* (New York: Fireside, 1994).
7. Jim Collins and Jerry I. Porras, *Built to Last: Successful Habits of Visionary Companies* (New York: HarperBusiness, 1994).
8. Jon Gordon, *The Power of a Positive Team: Proven Principles and Practices That Make Great Teams Great* (Hoboken, NJ: John Wiley & Sons, 2018).
9. Blake Mycoskie, *Start Something That Matters* (New York: Spiegel & Grau, 2011), 32.

Acknowledgments

Three people's efforts stood out in the writing and editing process, and they deserve special thanks: Carol Traver—for shaping, guiding, massaging, cajoling, and at times completely rewriting parts of the raw manuscript to help us achieve what we'd set out to do; Kim Miller—for her editing assistance in making us sound smarter than we are, for climbing so far into the weeds of the book that she realized we had the Vipers playing seventeen games . . . or maybe sixteen (who could be sure?), and for letting Nathan complain about semicolons; and Scott Whitaker—for his edits, comments, and guidance on the latest research about high-impact teams.

ABOUT THE AUTHORS

Tony Dungy is a #1 *New York Times* bestselling author whose books include *Quiet Strength, Uncommon, The Mentor Leader,* and *Uncommon Marriage* (with Lauren Dungy). He led the Indianapolis Colts to a Super Bowl victory on February 4, 2007, the first such win for an African American head coach. Dungy established another NFL first by becoming the first head coach to lead his teams to the playoffs for ten consecutive years.

Dungy joined the Colts in 2002 after serving as the most successful head coach in Tampa Bay Buccaneers history. He has also held assistant coaching positions with the University of Minnesota, Pittsburgh Steelers, Kansas City Chiefs, and Minnesota Vikings. Before becoming a coach, he played three seasons in the NFL. Dungy was inducted into the Pro Football Hall of Fame in 2016.

Dungy has been involved in a wide variety of charitable organizations, including All Pro Dad, Abe Brown Ministries, Fellowship of Christian Athletes, Athletes in Action, Mentors for Life, Big Brothers Big Sisters, and Boys & Girls Clubs. He has also worked with Basket of Hope, Impact for Living, the Black Coaches Association National Convention, Indiana Black

Expo, the United Way of Central Indiana, and the American Diabetes Association. He retired from coaching in 2009 and now serves as a studio analyst for NBC's *Football Night in America*. He and his wife, Lauren, are the parents of ten children.

Nathan Whitaker lives in Florida with his wife and two daughters. After graduating from Harvard Law School, he worked in football administration for the Jacksonville Jaguars and Tampa Bay Buccaneers. In addition to writing, Nathan also speaks on topics relevant to corporations, churches, and sports teams, and is a cofounder of Impact for Living.

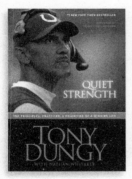
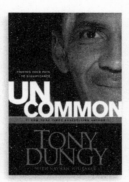
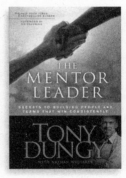
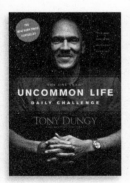
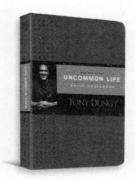
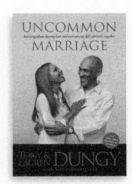

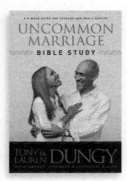

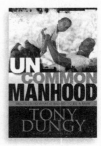

The Uncommon
Marriage Adventure
(with Lauren Dungy)

Uncommon Marriage
Bible Study
(with Lauren Dungy)

Uncommon Manhood
(Gift book)

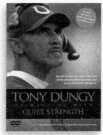

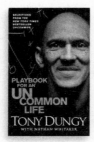

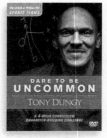

Tony Dungy on
Winning with Quiet
Strength (DVD)

Playbook for an
Uncommon Life
(6-pack for groups)

Dare to Be
Uncommon
(DVD curriculum)

THE UNCOMMON LIFE
WEEKLY CHALLENGE (E-BOOKS)

Developing Your Core   Strengthening Your Family

Building Your Team   Achieving Your Potential

Living Your Life's Purpose   Maximizing Your Influence

Strengthening Your Faith

QUIET STRENGTH and **DARE TO BE UNCOMMON** men's Bible studies
are available from Group Publishing (www.group.com).